It's Quite OK to Walk Away

It's Quite OK to Walk Away

A review of the UK's Brexit options
with the help of seven international databases

Michael Burrage

CIVITAS

First published April 2017

© Civitas 2017
55 Tufton Street
London SW1P 3QL

email: books@civitas.org.uk

ISBN 978-1-906837-85-3

Independence: Civitas: Institute for the Study of Civil
Society is a registered educational charity (No. 1085494)
and a company limited by guarantee (No. 04023541).
Civitas is financed from a variety of private sources to
avoid over-reliance on any single or small group of donors.
All publications are independently refereed.

All the Institute's publications seek to further its objective
of promoting the advancement of learning. The views
expressed are those of the authors, not of the Institute, as is
responsibility for data and content.

Designed and typeset by Typetechnique

Printed in Great Britain by
4edge Limited, Essex

Contents

Author   ix

Acknowledgements   x

Summary   xi

1. A key decision is taken, but many questions remain   1

2. There has been no authoritative UK analysis   5

3. Untrustworthy estimates from the Treasury   9

4. An extrapolation - what might have happened without the Single Market?   15

5. Top 40 fastest-growing goods exporters to the Single Market   18

6. How have exporters to the EU under WTO rules performed?   24

7. A closer look at the impact of EU trade agreements   28

8. A synoptic view of trading with the EU under four different relationships   30

9. How has UK fared when exporting under WTO rules?   39

10. Scotch versus Bourbon: exports of an EU member and a 'most favoured nation'   41

11. Strange Brexiteer arguments against trading under WTO rules   47

12. Does a single market in services exist?   52

13. Top 40 fastest-growing service exporters   57
    to the EU28

14. Members or non-members, who benefits most   60
    from the single market in services?

15. Have Swiss services exports suffered outside   63
    the Single Market?

16. The big 'known unknown': passports, clearing   65
    and other financial services

17. Other dashed hopes and unfounded claims: 75
    the Single Market in retrospect

18. A summary of the evidence   92

19. Conclusions   101

20. Notes on the negotiations   103

Appendices

I.   Comments on *HM Treasury analysis:*   113
     the long-term economic impact of EU
     membership and the alternatives

II. On the role of trade associations in a   120
     post-Brexit trade intelligence network

III. On the Scottish Government's puzzling   138
     enthusiasm for membership of the Single Market

Notes   146

Author

Michael Burrage is a director of Cimigo, which is based in Ho Chi Minh City, Vietnam, and conducts market and corporate strategy research in China, India and 12 countries in the Asia Pacific region. He is also a founder director of a start-up specialist telecom company which provides the free telephone interpreter service for aid workers and others where interpreters are scarce. He is a sociologist by training, was a Fulbright scholar at the University of Pennsylvania, has been a lecturer at the London School of Economics and at the Institute of United States Studies, specialising in the comparative analysis of industrial enterprise and professional institutions. He has been a research fellow at Harvard, at the Swedish Collegium of Advanced Study, Uppsala, at the Free University of Berlin, and at the Center for Higher Education Studies and the Institute of Government of the University of California, Berkeley. He has also been British Council lecturer at the University of Pernambuco, Recife, Brazil, and on several occasions a visiting professor in Japan, at the universities of Kyoto, Hokkaido and Kansai and at Hosei University in Tokyo. He has written articles in American, European and Japanese sociological journals, conducted a comparative study of telephone usage in Tokyo, Manhattan, Paris and London for NTT, and a study of British entrepreneurs for Ernst & Young. His publications include *Revolution and the Making of the Contemporary Legal Profession: England, France and the United States* (OUP, 2006) and *Class Formation, Civil Society and the State: A comparative analysis of Russia, France, the United States and England* (Palgrave Macmillan, 2008). He edited *Martin Trow: Twentieth-century higher education: from elite to mass to universal* (Johns Hopkins, 2010).

His previous Civitas publications include *Where's the Insider Advantage? A review of the evidence that withdrawal from the EU would not harm the UK's exports or foreign investment in the UK* (July 2014); 'A club of high and severe unemployment: the Single Market over the 21 years 1993-2013' (July 2015) in the Europe Debate series; *Myth and Parodox of the Single Market: How the trade benefits of EU membership have been mis-sold* (January 2016); and *The Eurosceptic's Handbook: 50 live issues in the Brexit debate* (May 2016).

Acknowledgements

I have to thank the Civitas team for their help in retrieving data for this book, and in particular to Justin Protts, who helped enormously in searching and critically evaluating sources, and in the presentation of the data. I also benefited from the comments of a blind reviewer, and am rather sorry that it is not the custom to publish them along with an author's replies. Conversations on related topics extending back over many years, with Kevin Lewis were invariably stimulating and helpful. They have all done their best to correct my mistakes. I am solely responsible for those that remain.

Civitas is very grateful to the Nigel Vinson Charitable Trust for its generous support of this project.

Summary

The image of the EU's Single Market as an economically successful project, and as 'a vital national interest' for the UK, has rested on the hopes and repeated assurances of leading politicians, on a sympathetic media, and on the occasional endorsements of individual companies, rather than on any credible evidence about its benefits for the UK economy as a whole.

No UK government over the past 23 years has sought to monitor its impact until the rushed analysis of HM Treasury published just before the referendum. On many counts, this was an unreliable and untrustworthy document. There is, therefore, no authoritative evidence to enable one to assess the economic consequences of the government's decision to leave the Single Market, or of any future agreement it might negotiate, or of a decision to leave with no deal and to trade with the EU under World Trade Organization (WTO) rules.

Seven international databases are used in this report to assess the benefits of the Single Market for the UK, and to compare its performance with that of other EU members, and with non-members who have traded with the EU either as members of the European Economic Area (EEA), or under bilateral agreements or as WTO members.

The key metric in this report is the growth of exports, since that is what the Single Market was expected to deliver for the UK, and is often thought to have delivered. The data presented shows, by multiple measures, that this has not happened. By comparison with the Common Market decades from 1973 to 1992, the Single Market years from 1993 to 2015 have been an era of declining UK export growth to the EU. When ranked among the top 40 fastest-growing exporters to the other founder members of the Single Market the

UK comes 36th. It has been surpassed by numerous countries trading with the EU under WTO rules. Moreover, the growth of UK exports to the 111 countries, with which it has itself traded under WTO rules since 1993, has been four times greater than that of its exports to the EU.

Over the 43 years of EU membership, UK exports of goods to 11 long-standing members of the EU have grown just two per cent more, and at a compound annual growth rate (CAGR) just 0.02 percentage points higher, than 14 countries trading under WTO rules. EU12 exports to each other have grown just 1 per cent more than the exports of these 14 countries. In other words, the growth of goods exports of the UK to 11 long-standing members of the EU over these 43 years are barely distinguishable from those of 14 countries exporting under WTO rules, and they of course have not incurred any of the costs of EU membership.

Over the 23 years of the Single Market, however, exports from these same 14 countries have grown 27 per cent *more* than exports from the UK, at a CAGR that is 0.93 points higher. Norway and Iceland, members of the EEA, and Switzerland and Turkey, which have had bilateral agreements with EU over most of these years, have performed similarly and very much better than the EU members and the UK.

Overall, the cross-national data on goods exports lends strong support to the UK Government's decision to leave the Single Market, and to seek a comprehensive bilateral free trade agreement. However, the experience of 14 countries that have been trading with the EU under WTO rules also offers reassurance to the UK negotiators who may have to decide that no deal is better than the bad deal they have been offered by the EU. Their experience suggests that leaving the EU with no deal and thereafter trading with it under WTO rules will be an acceptable option for the UK, even though the UK exporters will have to adjust to customs procedures that those 14 countries have grown used to over the past 23 years.

The more time-limited data available about services exports show that a Single Market in services, as measured by the European Commission's preferred index of the difference between intra and extra-EU exports as a proportion of GDP, could barely be said to exist having reached its high point in 2007. It has not grown since. In a ranking of the top 40 fastest-growing service exporters to the EU15 between 2010 and 2014, the UK finishes 25th place and has again been surpassed by many non-EU members. The mean rate of intra-EU export growth of EU members from 2004 to 2012 was *lower* than the rate of growth of the services exports of 27 non-members to the EU. Since a Single Market in services barely exists, there is little to be lost by leaving it.

National aggregate statistics may, however, hide sectors that have benefited from Single Market directives. Banking is the notable example since passports authorised under several EU directives enable banks to trade anywhere in the EU. Estimates show that, in the absence of a specific agreement, there is a risk of a significant decline in the pan-EU services of UK-based banks. These estimates are, however, unable to say how far alternatives, such as subsidiaries or access by third countries deemed equivalent, would reduce or eliminate these risks. Aviation is another service sector that might suffer from leaving the Single Market, though the probability of leaving without some agreement on this is considerably lower.

The evidence in these databases suggests that the other supposed benefits of the Single Market are largely imaginary. There is, for example, no evidence that Single Market membership has had a positive impact on UK GDP or productivity growth, one of the main expectations both of EEC membership and of the Single Market. Though much-praised, the EU's external trade agreements could not have been of much benefit to the UK, since by 2014 they covered such tiny proportions of UK world exports, 6.1 per cent of goods and 1.8 per cent of services. The idea that the Single Market has been good for jobs is belied by the astonishing employment record of the 12 founder members when compared with other OECD members. Since 1993, the Single Market has been a club of distinctively high, distinctively severe, long-term unemployment which has normalised previously unthinkable levels of unemployment, especially among 15 to 24-year-olds. The record of the EU's later entrants is still worse.

It is extremely difficult to determine whether Single Market membership has boosted foreign direct investment (FDI) in the UK. Since 2007, the European Commission has itself been concerned about the failure of the Single Market to attract international investment, and it has not revived, as it has in many other areas, since the financial crisis. The mean value of FDI stock of EU members is low by comparison with many independent countries, which does not suggest that EU membership per se has been a powerful attraction.

Overall, the evidence shows that the disadvantages of non-membership of the EU and Single Market have been vastly exaggerated and that the supposed benefits of membership, whether for exports of goods and services, for productivity, for world-wide trade, or for employment, are largely imaginary. The Government appears to have decided to leave the Single Market on the basis that we should return full control of UK laws to the UK, but trade data also offers strong support for the decision, and provides comfort for those worried about relying on WTO rules if no deal emerges. The benefits of EU and Single Market membership have been illusory, while its costs are real, onerous, and unacceptable to a majority of the British people.

The report ends with comments on the negotiations. The first three moves are already known: leaving the Single Market, offering free trade, and passing a Great Repeal Bill to incorporate into UK law all current EU regulations, procedures and rules governing trade. All of which may be amended as deemed necessary sometime in the future. This will ensure a high degree of continuity in the conduct of trade, and drastically reduce the required scope in the negotiation of an EU-UK trade agreement. Indeed, much of that agreement is in effect already written since customs on both sides of the Channel are already applying exactly the same rules.

There was a hint of a fourth move in the Prime Minister's comment that 'no deal is better than a bad deal', intimating that the UK is ready to walk away without a deal. Since, as just mentioned, the experience of countries that have long traded with the EU under WTO rules show this is an acceptable solution for the UK, the UK negotiators might be advised to state a deadline beyond which date, if no agreement can be reached, the UK will trade under WTO rules. This might prevent delay being used as a bargaining device or to punish the UK.

Beyond issues of trade barriers other issues should not cause significant trouble. Migration should not be a relevant issue in these negotiations, other than providing guarantees to UK and EU residents on both sides. A method of adjudicating disputes will be required, but this can be lifted from that already agreed with Canada or the United States. The UK will also offer to contribute to, and participate in, various EU agencies and programmes of its choice, to demonstrate that it is ready to remain a friendly neighbour, but these need not form part of the trade negotiations, and can continue long after Brexit.

Once the unique character of the trade negotiations between the two parties is recognised, there is little reason why a slimline trade agreement cannot be concluded well before 30th September 2018, the date by which EU's chief Brexit negotiator, Michel Barnier, wants to wrap up the terms of Britain's exit from the Union.

Given the UK's bargaining position in favour of free trade, managed immigration, continued co-operation with EU agencies and programmes, there is no need for secrecy about its basic principles and positions. On the contrary, the UK has much to gain, if they are widely publicised across the EU and the UK. They might elicit support from EU exporters, and even from Remainers at home, for whom free trade is, one imagines, the main merit of the Single Market. UK negotiators might also escape some of the blame, if tariffs and restrictions are required after all.

1

A key decision is taken, but many questions remain

On 17th January 2017, the Prime Minister declared unequivocally that the UK would not seek to remain a member of the Single Market when it withdrew from the EU. Clearly, in not so many words, the grounds for this decision were primarily because the UK government did not wish to accept freedom of movement, or the authority of the European Court of Justice (ECJ), while EU leaders consider these are fundamental principles of the Single Market, on which there can be no compromise.

> European leaders have said many times that membership means accepting the 'four freedoms' of goods, capital, services and people. And being out of the EU but a member of the Single Market would mean complying with the EU's rules and regulations that implement those freedoms, without having a vote on what those rules and regulations are. It would mean accepting a role for the European Court of Justice that would see it still having direct legal authority in our country. It would to all intents and purposes mean not leaving the EU at all … So we do not seek membership of the Single Market … But I respect the position taken by European leaders who have been clear about their position, just as I am clear about mine.

Later, when referring to the prospect of new trade agreements with other countries, she observed that 'since joining the EU, trade as a percentage of GDP has broadly stagnated in the UK'. In this context therefore, economic calculations became relevant, but the question of Single Market membership had already been decided by the incompatible red lines.

They have, however, played a much larger part in the arguments of opponents of the government decision. They are mentioned first among the Liberal Democrats' reasons for remaining a member of the Single Market, even though they have not yet conducted any serious research to support their argument.[1] Perhaps they will do so, if there is a second referendum. The Scottish Government has strongly opposed a 'hard' Brexit and trading under WTO rules, an option Mrs May specifically left on the table, after stating her preference for a comprehensive reciprocal free trade deal, by saying that 'no deal for Britain is better than a bad deal'. In the view of the Scottish Government, trading under WTO rules 'would severely damage Scotland's economic, social and cultural interests' and 'hit jobs and living standards – deeply and permanently'.[2] It therefore argued, not yet very persuasively it must be said, that for economic reasons Scotland should remain in Single Market, after the rest of the UK leaves. They are, however, conducting 'sectoral studies' which may make a stronger case, and presumably, will be published in due course.

On the 7th October 2016, the heads of four UK industrial federations, the Confederation of British Industry (CBI), the Engineering Employers' Federation (EEF), the International Chamber of Commerce (ICC), and techUK, published an open letter to the Prime Minister which said:

> Every credible study that has been conducted has shown that this WTO option would do serious and lasting damage to the UK economy and those of our trading partners. The Government should give certainty to business by immediately ruling this option out under any circumstances.[3]

Since it is difficult to think of any credible studies of the WTO option might mean for UK trade with the EU, I asked all four of these associations for the names of any of these studies, but they all declined to name any of them.

In June 2015, a year before the referendum, a *Financial Times* (*FT*) columnist, Wolfgang Münchau, observed that

> ...if you look at the trend of EU-wide productivity, the single market leaves no trace ... It has been downhill ever since the official start date of the single market in 1992. Productivity trends in Britain are

very similar. You could, of course, argue that without the single market, the situation might have been worse, but that assertion is impossible to prove. My point is that the single market is not visible in the macro statistics. What you are hearing are extrapolations from a micro perspective. Advocates of the single market might benefit from it personally, and so might their shareholders and employees. But the data are telling us a different story – that the single market is a giant economic non-event, for both the EU and the UK.[4]

He ended up saying he found it 'hard to make a compelling case for British membership of the EU on the grounds of the single market' and he would 'go further and reject all utilitarian arguments.'

In September 2016, another *FT* columnist, Martin Wolf, whipped his readers into a frenzy after saying:

I would like a government prepared to overturn the referendum ... the UK is making a huge economic and strategic blunder. The country is going to be meaner and poorer ... what now has to be done is to move to the miserable new dispensation as smoothly as possible.[5]

Most of those who commented on his article seemed to have believed that the UK was about to lose some priceless national asset, though what exactly that was Wolf did not think it necessary to say. He had, on previous occasions, predicted these to be a loss of trade, a fall in GDP and incomes, a rise in unemployment, a fall in foreign and domestic investment, and increased borrowing costs. All together therefore, his post-Brexit UK seemed a bleak and depressing place. Not surprisingly, bloggers took his cue and expressed their anger and distress through abuse of leave voters as easily fooled illiterates, narrow-minded xenophobes, racists, and so forth, who wanted to take us there. So even within the small and moderately informed community of *FT* readers, rational and courteous debate collapsed.

Mrs May expressed hope that 'after all the division and discord, the country is coming together'. But it hardly seems likely that reasonable and courteous debate about her decision to leave the Single Market will resume if there is still no evidence to help us decide whether the Single Market has been 'a giant non-event' or whether leaving it is 'a huge strategic and economic blunder' and 'likely to do serious and lasting damage to the UK economy'. Thus far, the only attempt from the Government to evaluate the Single Market in comparison with other post-Brexit trade relationships with the EU, under a bilateral agreement or trading under WTO rules, are the model-based predictions of UK GDP and household incomes in 2030 provided by the Treasury during the referendum campaign. By these calculations continued membership of the Single Market, via continued membership of the EEA, was much the best option, and trading under WTO rules much the worst.

For reasons explained in some detail below, these Treasury predictions cannot, however, be taken as the last word on these relationships. This research tries to identify their relative merits and demerits in a different manner. It draws on the best available evidence from seven international databases to analyse UK economic performance, and especially in exporting, as a member of the Single Market, and compares it with that of countries that have been trading under different relationships over the same period. It is an evaluation based on past performance which, as it happens, did not feature greatly in the referendum debate. Both sides preferred to work with rosy, or grim, predictions.

There are reasons, however, for thinking that the historical record will provide a more reliable and trustworthy guide than model-based predictions. The directors of these international agencies may well have personal views about the merits of the EU or the Single Market, but it seems unlikely that these had any influence whatever on their record-keepers who have been conscientiously entering trade data over the past four decades. It has another advantage – all the sources used are publicly accessible and verifiable. The model-based estimates and predictions of the Treasury rest on equations, proxies, assumptions and calculations which can be evaluated by a rather small number of people, and in all probability these do not include the politicians and journalists who rushed to make use of them in the Remain cause. The databases used in this analysis are, by contrast, publicly available websites. The peer review of the Treasury analysis is a tiny band of fellow specialists. The peer review of this analysis is open to everyone with access to the internet.

2

There has been no authoritative UK analysis

As soon as we start to search for the past benefits for the UK, of EU or Single Market membership, we have to face the surprising and inconvenient fact that, over the entire 43 years of membership of the EU and the European Economic Community (EEC), the Government never sought to regularly monitor and analyse their benefits and costs. They evidently did not consider this to be their responsibility. Since John Major, successive prime ministers seem to have thought that it was their task to persuade the British people of the benefits of EU and Single Market membership, and that this might best be done by repeatedly commending these benefits rather than by actually measuring them. None of them instructed the Treasury or the Department for Business to collect data about UK performance within the Single Market and to publish regular assessments, or even to analyse the data being routinely collected by international agencies, such as the United Nations (UN), the International Monetary Fund (IMF), the Organisation for Economic Co-operation and Development (OECD), the World Bank or the WTO.

The European Commission shared this reluctance. It first officially raised the question 'Can we measure the performance of the Single Market?' not in January 1993 when it formally began, but almost 22 years later, in June 2014. The Internal Market Committee of the European Parliament met to consider this question. Then it identified ways in which this might be done at some point in the future, but did not offer an answer. For undisclosed reasons, it ruled out 'economic indicators for a country-based annual assessment' as if it did not want individual member countries to be able to assess the merits and demerits of membership for themselves.[1]

Other long-term advocates of EU membership in the UK have behaved in a similar manner, as if constant affirmation of its success and benefits made empirical verification unnecessary. It is worth giving some examples since they illustrate a rather remarkable social phenomenon – an idea remaining aloft, and gathering numerous adherents, supported by nothing more than hopes, impressions, media bites and hot air. Even if the benefits of the Single Market were eventually found to be supported by rock solid empirical evidence, it would be no less remarkable that for so long it has not needed it.

Nick Clegg, as a former employee of the Commission and a former MEP, must have known all the right sources, contacts and experts to document its benefits. As a columnist of *The Guardian*, the paper of the social research community, he had time to explain them to a receptive and knowledgeable audience. However, in his 198 columns, in various newspapers since 2001 he never once did so, referring on one occasion to its 'untold benefits', which he declined to tell us about, and on another to 'immeasurable benefits' which therefore seemed therefore to excuse him from making any attempt to measure them.[2]

Kenneth Clarke, a former chancellor, forever ready with an enthusiastic soundbite on behalf of the EU, gave a speech in 2013 entitled 'It is time to put the European Case more strongly'. Those recalling only his soundbites might have agreed, but 'more strongly' in his mind evidently meant more emphatically or insistently, rather than with more convincing evidence. In any event, he closed by declaring that 'the benefits we reap from it are quite astonishing', but without identifying any of them.[3]

Sir Richard Lambert, former director general of the CBI and editor of the *Financial Times* – both roles that might have presented opportunities to initiate research to identify and measure the benefits of the EU – opened a lecture in 2013 saying: 'I want to base my arguments as far as is possible on evidence.' However, having repeated various familiar claims about the EU, he decided halfway through that it wasn't really possible and that 'the truth is, that it's just as difficult to calculate the benefits as it is the costs of EU membership to us all'. Is it? Should we not even try? Was there no one at the *FT* who could analyse the evidence in the OECD, IMF and other databases that had been publicly available for years?

By the time of the referendum campaign, the advocates of membership seem to have grown accustomed to this form of proof by affirmation and reiteration. Mr Cameron's favourite slogan was that the EU was 'good for trade, investment, and jobs', but he never pointed to a single empirical analysis which supported his belief. A good number of individual companies and trade associations added their endorsements, and no doubt credibility, but these were equally devoid of empirical evidence, and so it was not until almost the last moment that the Treasury produced a report, containing what looked like empirical research. Up to that point, the Remain campaign's argument rested, as it had always done, on the high *proportion* of UK exports going to the other 27 countries and a high proportion of every country's exports goes to their closest 27 neighbours. Moreover, the relative share of the value of UK goods exports going to the EU, while growing sharply during the Common Market decades from 1973 to 1992, has declined over the life of the Single Market from about 54 per cent to just below 44 per cent.[4] Forty-four per cent is still, of course, a high proportion, but it says nothing whatever about how the Single Market might have helped those exports.

Two reports from the Treasury sought to make good this deficiency. Not by analysing the record of what had actually happened to the UK economy during the years of membership of the EU and Single Market. Instead, by using a VAR model to make predictions of the immediate consequences of a vote to leave, and a gravity model to make long-term predictions of the losses that UK trade and therefore GDP would sustain over the next 15 years after it left the EU.[5] The latter is of particular interest here since to predict what UK trade with the EU will be when it is not a member of the EU or the Single Market, it necessarily had to calculate what the benefits of membership of both have been thus far. It is those supposed benefits that we hope to identify.

Before examining what the Treasury thinks those benefits have been, it is worth noting that it does not quote or cite a single earlier study of benefits for the UK economy since the Single Market began – thus confirming that the widely held notion of the success of the Single Market must have been based up to that point on something other than empirical evidence.[6] Did the Treasury finally provide that evidence, on 13th April 2016, just two months before the referendum?

3

Untrustworthy estimates from the Treasury

Opinions differ about the value of the predictions from the two Treasury models. Martin Wolf in the *Financial Times* took them as gospel, as official reports which ought to be reported as news, accepted and used to rebut what he called Project Lie of the Brexiteers. On the grounds that he knew the Treasury to be eurosceptic (he did not say whether he included the then chancellor) he argued that they had understated the problems of falling GDP and rising unemployment after Brexit. He therefore felt he should add a few predictions of his own, among them a collapse of foreign direct investment (FDI), so that 'the final outcome might well prove devastating'.[1] No wonder his readers were both angry and excitable on 24th June.

His *FT* colleague, Wolfgang Münchau, treated all these predictions as 'highly speculative and almost certainly wrong'. Moreover, the entire effort was, he thought, inappropriate: 'Macroeconomic modelling has many useful roles. But it is an abuse of the methodology and the underlying mathematical assumptions to pretend that one can gauge the long-term economic consequences of an unknown political decision.'[2]

The most comprehensive and detailed critique came from a fellow econometrician, David Blake.[3] He identified: all the questionable assumptions built into the Treasury model, such as that the shock of a Brexit vote would equal half of that of the financial crisis and last for two years; its failure to consider any alternative outcomes, such as that the Government might respond to the shock of the vote and Brexit, or might negotiate other effective trade arrangements;

and its reluctance, in defiance of all the accepted norms of scientific research, to consider other models whose predictions differed widely from its own. In the end, he came to the view that the two reports were 'two of the most ridiculous and excruciatingly awful official documents I have ever read' and 'an embarrassment to the economic profession'.

In the present context, however, the predictions of future losses to UK GDP and UK households are of less interest than the Treasury estimates of the past benefits of EU and Single Market membership. After citing four academic estimates of the gains in trade for the EU as a whole attributable to the EU membership, ranging from 51 per cent to 104 per cent, the Treasury decided that EU membership 'increases trade with EU members by somewhere between 68 per cent and 85 per cent' or 'by around three quarters.'[4]

Actually, this estimate, the major finding of the entire exercise, on which all the Treasury estimates about the past and future benefits of EU membership rest, is rather misleading as it merges the separate estimates of the benefits for goods and services. These separate estimates are not presented in full by the Treasury, but can be worked out from the coefficients they present in an appendix as a boost to trade in goods of 115.1 per cent and to services of 24.1 per cent.[5]

This means that the Treasury's estimate of the boost to goods trade from EU membership is an outlier, rather than reassuringly in the middle of the other estimates it chose to mention.[6] Moreover, the most recent of the cited studies decided that 'in linear model estimates, the accession to the Single Market is found to have *a large impact on trade [in goods] with all OECD partners, but without any specific impact on trade within EEA members on top of the overall impact*'. It went on to say, however, that 'alternative estimates with the Poisson model show that the positive impact is concentrated on trade within the EEA. All in all, various specifications converge to show an overall impact of EEA accession of roughly 60 per cent gains in trade intensity; *albeit it is not clear whether this is mainly a trade gain within the area or with all partners.*' The added italics highlight that this study can hardly be said to corroborate the Treasury estimate of 115.1 per cent boost to trade in goods from EU or EEA membership. Indeed, it might better be seen as a warning of the uncertainty surrounding all the claims about the impact of Single Market membership on the trade of its members.

If this estimate of 115.1 per cent boost to the trade in goods of EU members, including the UK, was anywhere near the truth for the UK, and not distorted by the accession of many post-socialist states, we would have to conclude that Mrs May and the Government had made a serious misjudgement. In such a case, remain critics might genuinely have a strong case.[7] Thus, it is important, to say the least, to decide whether we should believe the Treasury.

Although the Treasury cited no earlier studies about the benefits of the Single Market for the UK economy, it forgot to mention that it had itself conducted some research on the impact of the Single Market in 2005, which is publicly known only because of a freedom of information request in 2010. In that paper the Treasury estimated that EU 'membership initially boosted UK trade with the EU by seven per cent' while the Single Market had, it claimed, been able 'to boost intra-EU trade by a further nine per cent', but it added hopefully that this nine per cent 'may be an under-estimate'.[8] It went on to express surprise that 'after this initial boost from accession, straightforward comparisons of UK trade with the EU15 and the rest of the world from 1970 to date do not immediately highlight the significant boost in trade amongst the EEC members that one might have expected, particularly over the period of implementation of the Single Market.'

In this study, the Treasury noticed that trade between EU member states as a whole had been boosted by more than four times as much as that of the UK, 'by 38 per cent' rather than nine per cent. It then suggested that this might be due to 'the fact that the UK was more open to trade than some member states before accession, and therefore the relative impact may have been less'.[9]

It is understandable that the Treasury decided not to refer back to its own 2005 estimate, since they would then have had to explain why, having failed to identify any significant boost to intra-EU trade in 2005, and despite the known decline in the proportion of UK trade in goods with the EU since that date, it believed that EU membership could nevertheless have somehow boosted trade by 'three quarters' over the following decade, and trade in goods by a truly remarkable 115 per cent. Unfortunately, this breach of research etiquette is followed by others, and by a succession of mistakes, part methodological and part ethical, which render all the Treasury estimates totally unacceptable.

These mistakes are worth detailed analysis. They are itemized and explained in Appendix I. However, the most puzzling aspect of the Treasury analysis is that it never felt obliged, as many model builders do, to look out of the window and re-enter the real world to confirm that it had not lost all contact with it, and that their predictions are 'plausible', a common word in such exercises. They were content to let their model have the last word. The decline in UK goods exports to the EU from 2006 to 2015 from 54 per cent to 44 per cent, for example, is not consistent with their gravity model, but they chose not mention it, nor even to try to explain it.[10]

In their claim about the 75 per cent boost to UK trade, and the 115 percent boost to its trade in goods alone, from EU membership, they are of course making a claim about something that has actually happened, about which there is recorded evidence. We know, for instance, that UK goods exports to the other 11 founder members of the Single Market were valued at $176.85 billion in 2015, and since 1973 have grown at an annual real rate (CAGR) of 2.65 per cent.[11] If the UK had remained *outside* the EU and their goods exports had not been boosted by 115 per cent from EU membership, their value, according to the Treasury model, would have been somewhere around $82 billion in 2015. The real annual growth rate since 1973 would then have been 0.79 per cent. However, we also know that UK exports to countries across the world grew, over these same 43 years, despite all the tariff and non-tariff barriers they faced, at a CAGR of 2.35 per cent.

It is implausible, to say the least, that the growth of UK exports to the rest of the world would have been so much higher than that to near-neighbours, merely because the UK had decided to remain a member of EFTA, rather than joining the EEC in 1973. If it had, it would directly contradict the fundamental proposition on which their model and all their estimates rest, namely, that trade between countries varies inversely with their distance from one another.

The Treasury estimates necessarily assume that, had the UK not joined in 1973, a truly extraordinary decline in UK export growth to the EEC/EU countries post-1973 would have occurred. Over the years of EFTA membership from 1960 to 1972, UK exports to the six founder members of the EU grew at a real CAGR of 4.31 per cent, and to the future EU12 at a rate of 7.45 per cent.[12] The Treasury felt no need to explain why it is likely that, as a member of EFTA, the latter rate would have fallen to just 0.79 per cent.

Plainly, a better starting point for estimating what the EU and Single Market might have contributed to UK exports would have been the difference between the rate of growth of UK exports to it from 1973 to 2015 (2.65 per cent) versus export growth to the rest of the world over the same period (2.35 per cent) which is 0.30 per cent.[13] The gravity equation might then be used to decide what proportions of this 0.30 per cent superiority might be due to the in-built advantage of geographical proximity, or to the collapse of socialism and the entry to the EU of 11 post-socialist states, or to the other unsuspected benefits of the EU and the Single Market. The Treasury did not, however, care about such cross-checks. 'About three quarters' sounded good, or perhaps helpful, for the then chancellor, and some studies gave roughly similar answers, so they let it go.

Bearing in mind all the methodological flaws, including those listed in Appendix I, we must conclude that the Treasury estimate of the benefits of the Single Market is untrustworthy and implausible. Their model-building and analyses fell far short of normally acceptable research standards and perhaps for that reason were published anonymously. The Treasury seems to have forgotten that, as a major department of state engaged in advising the British people on a decision that will affect their livelihoods for generations to come, they have an obligation far above that to their temporary political masters. On this occasion, they declined to recognise any such obligation. On a previous occasion, they did not. At the time of the euro debate, they reached out across the world for the best economic advice available to determine whether or not the UK should join, invited critical commentaries, held seminars to cross-check and criticise submissions, and published in full the debate that preceded the then chancellor's decision.[14] In 2016 they failed to live up to their own standards and, one suspects, to most other people's. Though Martin Wolf of the *FT* seems to have found them acceptable.

These comments are, however, far from the last we will hear of the Treasury's claims. At many points, when reporting the evidence from the world's best databases, we have an opportunity to reconsider them, and to compare their estimates of the best and worst post-Brexit trading options with the past experience of numerous member and non-member countries.[15] If there is any substance or truth in their claims, it will necessarily emerge from this data. Somewhere or other, there will be indications of a 75 per cent boost to UK trade, or a 115 per cent boost to its goods trade, from EU membership. Somewhere there should be an indication of disadvantages the UK might suffer should it find itself to trade under WTO rules. They could hardly be hidden.

4

An extrapolation – what might have happened without the Single Market?

Before looking at this data, it is of interest to consider one very simple way of estimating what the Single Market might have contributed to UK goods exports. This is to extrapolate the rate of growth of UK exports to 11 other founder members of the Single Market during the two Common Market decades 1973 to 1992 over the real growth of UK exports under the Single Market from 1993 to 2015.[1] If the Single Market had boosted UK exports to fellow members in any respect, we might reasonably expect to see a surge or at any rate faster export growth over the Single Market years.

Two versions of an extrapolation are shown in Figure 4.1. The purple dashed line extends the exponential growth curve of actual export values from 1973 to 1992 over the years 1993 to 2015. It therefore shows what the growth of exports could have been over the years 1993 to 2015 if the Single Market had never been thought of, and all the factors that determined the rate of growth of exports in the Common Market decades had continued in exactly the same manner over the Single Market years. R^2 is the measure of fit of the trendline over the years from 1973 to 1992. The red dashed shows the linear trendline for 1973 to 1992 exports extended to 2015 and shows what would have happened had exports continued to rise by the same value each year continuing the trend from 1973 to 1992.

These, of course, are entirely imaginary reconstructions, but an interesting starting point. Far from showing any kind of visible benefit from membership of the Single Market, the line recording their actual growth over the Single Market decades (in blue) shows UK exports to these fellow members were significantly lower in 2015 than we might have expected. Exports are 69 per cent lower than if they had continued to grow at the same rate as they had done under the Common Market years and, astonishingly, 41 per cent lower than had exports just increased by the same amount year-on-year as they had done during the Common Market years.

Figure 4.1: UK goods exports to the 11 other founding members of the Single Market, 1973 to 2015 with linear and expotential trendline for 1973 to 1992 exports extended to 2015 in constant US (1973)$

Source: IMF Direction of Trade Statistics DOTS database (accessed at data.imf.org.uk on 06/11/2016)

The real growth rate of UK exports in the Common Market decades was 6.04 per cent, and in the 23 years of the Single Market was 1.00 per cent. This dismal performance is no doubt due in part to the financial crisis of 2008. Even if, for the sake of argument, we assume (what is by no means certain) that export growth during the pre-crisis boom was part of the normal growth path of the Single Market, CAGR over the 15 pre-crisis years to 2007 was 4.06 per cent. Therefore, still almost two per cent below that of the Common Market years.

By contrast, a similar analysis of the exports from nine non-EU OECD countries to the same 11 EU countries found that their exports over the pre-crisis years grew at a CAGR of 4.99 per cent which was faster than their 3.41 per cent growth over the Common Market years. However, they too experienced a sharp decline following the crisis, but their CAGR over the entire period from 1993 to 2015 was 2.65 percent, more than double the UK's 1.00 per cent.[2]

Somehow or other, therefore, the exports of these non-EU members appear to have benefited from the Single Market more than those of the UK. That is before any account has been taken of any of the costs of membership for the UK, annual contributions, regulation of its entire economy, free movement, and surrendering the right to make its own trade agreements and so forth. Non-EU OECD members have not paid any of these costs, nor have they helped to make any of the Single Market rules, but they have nevertheless enjoyed faster export growth to the Single Market.

This counter-intuitive and baffling result deserves the most careful investigation. It has never received it. Probably because the idea that the Single Market has been a great benefit to the UK, a success story, a vital national interest, the crown jewel of EU membership, has taken hold of sections of the UK political elite and its media, even though it has no support in the databases of UK goods exports. To treat an annual export growth rate of one per cent over 23 years as success is absurd, but to go on to urge the UK to negotiate to remain a member of this market, and to pay the price of doing so, is doubly so.

However, this analysis makes use of extrapolations of an imaginary set of circumstances, so we will now look at real world evidence about the UK and other countries' exports to the Single Market in more detail.

5

Top 40 fastest-growing goods exporters to the Single Market

As a first step, Table 5.1 shows the compound annual growth rate (CAGR) of the exports of goods over 23 years of the Single Market to the 14 founder and long-time members of all those countries whose exports exceeded $5 billion in 2015. They are ranked in terms of growth, and to EU14 rather than EU15 because exports to the UK are excluded from the calculation, so that we may treat the UK as an outsider exporting to the other members and compare its exports with non-members' to the same number of export markets.

This list is of course a mixed bag, of emerging economies, primary producers, semi-developed economies, as well as developed ones, large and small. It can only be a rough measure of export performance since these countries have such diverse export profiles. However, it serves a useful purpose in the context of present debates. It reminds us, first, that non-members have access to the Single Market, and second, it shows that membership does not ensure a higher rate of growth of exports to the Single Market than non-members.

The UK's exports are the third largest in value, but in terms of growth it has not done well over the past 23 years, as the earlier extrapolation suggested, and lies in 36th position. There is not much consolation to be had in the argument that UK growth is bound to be low because the value of its exports is so large, while some of these countries are bound to have high rates of growth because they start from next to nothing. During the Common Market decades the UK was not only the largest exporter to the EU, but also grew faster than many of the other large exporters of the

Table 5.1: Top 40 goods exporters to the EU14, 1993-2015, by real growth and value
*has a trade agreement of some kind in force with the EU

	CAGR % (1993 US$)	Exporting Country	Export Value 2015 (US$ billion)
1	27.5	Iraq	11.0
2	23.8	Qatar	5.5
3	21.0	Vietnam	23.1
4	19.7	Azerbaijan	5.7
5	17.0	Kazakhstan	13.2
6	13.1	China	252.9
7	10.8	Angola	7.1
8	10.6	Bangladesh	10.6
9	9.8	UAE	7.7
10	7.0	India	32.6
11	7.0	Russia	119.1
12	6.5	Ukraine*	7.2
13	6.3	Turkey*	42.5
14	5.7	Mexico*	13.6
15	5.4	Morocco*	11.9
16	4.8	Nigeria	16.4
17	4.1	Philippines	5.9
18	3.5	Chile*	7.0
19	3.4	Norway*	57.3
20	3.2	Malaysia	16.4
21	3.1	Tunisia*	9.6
22	3.1	Colombia*	5.2
23	3.1	Brazil	29.3
24	3.0	Korea*	26.1
25	2.8	Switzerland*	104.5
26	2.6	Thailand	15.8
27	2.6	Israel*	10.4
28	2.5	Algeria*	19.7
29	2.5	Indonesia	12.4
30	2.4	South Africa*	13.1
31	2.3	United States	206.5
32	2.3	Singapore	23.1
33	2.1	Canada	15.4
34	1.6	Saudi Arabia	19.2
35	1.0	Australia	6.3
36	**0.9**	**UK**	**188.1**
37	0.5	Hong Kong	31.5
38	0.4	Argentina	6.3
39	-1.6	Libya	7.4
40	-2.1	Japan	49.5

Source: IMF DOTS, data.imf.org, accessed 4/11/2016
South Africa growth CAGR calculated using EU14 imports data

era, such as the United States, Switzerland, Canada, Norway, South Africa, Australia, and Brazil, all seven of which have overtaken the UK during the Single Market years.[1]

The United States is an especially illuminating example. The total value of UK exports to the EEC edged ahead of those of the US in 1973, just as it joined, and continued to grow at a faster pace until 1992, when their value was just over 50 percentage points higher than that of the US. There was then no word of slow growth because of their high value. The year 1992 was, curiously enough, their high point relative to US exports.[2] The growth of UK exports has been falling ever since, and they are now, as the table shows, some way behind US exports, which have been both larger and faster growing.

Export growth, we may safely conclude, has not been one of the benefits of the Single Market for the UK. Countries exporting under WTO rules, like the US, do not appear to be at any great disadvantage. Why then do the leaders of opposition parties, and a few dissident Conservatives, argue that it is important, even vital, for the UK to negotiate to remain, by some means and at some cost, in the Single Market? Unfortunately, they have never explained its appeal and the media do not care to ask them.

Table 5.2 shows the CAGR of the goods exports of all 15 founder and long-term members of the Single Market to each other together with those of the other 15 G20 countries. It provides a view therefore of the contemporaneous performance of fellow members of the Single Market, and eliminates the smaller emerging countries from the comparison.

The figures speak largely for themselves. The UK has not performed well by comparison with its fellow members. Its CAGR is the second lowest. However, all the founder and long-term members, as a whole, have not performed particularly well in their own Single Market. Their CAGR of their exports to each other was 2.4 per cent, while that of the exports to them of the other G20 countries was 4.0 per cent.

The higher growth rate of the non-members reinforces the impression given by the preceding table that, in terms of export growth, non-members have been significantly greater beneficiaries

Table 5.2: Real growth of goods exports to the EU15, 1993-2015, 15 long-term members of the Single Market (shaded) compared with 15 non-EU members of the G20
*has a trade agreement of some kind in force with the EU

Exporting Country	CAGR % (1993 US$)	Exports Value 2015 (US$ billions)
China	13.3	312.6
Mexico*	7.1	19.8
India	7.0	41.5
Turkey*	6.8	53.0
Russia	6.4	126.6
Netherlands	4.1	389.0
Spain	3.8	164.7
Canada	3.4	27.9
Korea*	3.4	34.0
Brazil	3.0	32.2
Portugal	2.9	37.9
Belgium	2.9	267.4
Luxembourg	2.9	13.2
Ireland	2.8	62.2
Austria	2.7	77.1
Germany	2.6	600.3
Sweden	2.4	72.1
Indonesia	2.1	13.9
United States	2.1	262.9
South Africa*	1.9	16.4
Denmark	1.4	51.8
Saudi Arabia	1.3	21.4
Italy	1.2	206.0
Finland	1.2	29.5
France	1.1	269.8
United Kingdom	**0.9**	**188.1**
Argentina	0.7	7.1
Australia	0.4	9.1
Greece	0.3	10.0
Japan	-2.2	60.2
EU CAGR 2.4%		
Non-EU CAGR 4.0%		

Source: IMF DOTS (accessed at data.imf.org on 06/11/2016)

of exporting to the Single Market than its own members. The export benefits of membership are proving much more difficult to identify than the Treasury suggested.

In an attempt to identify the disadvantages of non-membership for goods exporters, further comparisons were made with two other non-member 'groups' – all other OECD countries, and all big exporters to the EU15 (that is, countries whose exports to the EU in 2015 exceeded $20 billion – an arbitrary ceiling intended to exclude the remaining small and medium-sized, and often fast-growing, exporters who have entered global trading networks relatively recently).

In Figure 5.1 the growth of the goods exports of the EU15 to each other over 23 years of the Single Market is compared with that of these three comparator 'groups'; the other G20 countries included in Table 5.2, all other OECD countries, and countries who exported over $20 billion in goods to the EU in 2015.[3]

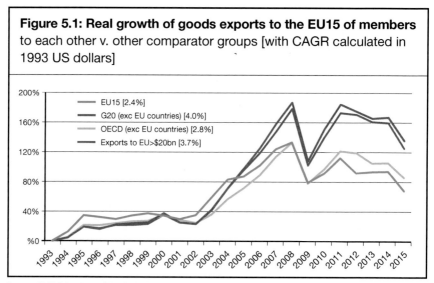

Figure 5.1: Real growth of goods exports to the EU15 of members to each other v. other comparator groups [with CAGR calculated in 1993 US dollars]

Source: IMF Direction of Trade Statistics. Missing values for reported exports to EU countries have been estimated by using the corresponding import data from the IMF DOTS database (accessed at data.imf. org on 06/11/2016).

By 2015, the total growth of both the G20 and of the exporters of over $20 billion in goods to the EU was approximately double that of the EU15 to each other. The growth for other OECD countries, excluding all EU members, was only 85 per cent versus the EU15's 67 per cent.

From whatever angle one looks, it is difficult to see any sign of what EU members might have gained from their membership of the Single Market, from all the time sitting and talking, from all the money spent, from all the EC directives and regulations to achieve a level playing field. There is no sign of the 115 per cent boost to the trade in goods of all members claimed by the Treasury model builders. Nor is there any sign of all the disadvantages that non-members were supposed to suffer as a result of the tariff and non-tariff barriers they have faced. At some point, hopefully in the not-too-distant future, the mixed band of politicians, Labour, Lib Dem, SNP, and dissident Tories, who are still arguing that the UK should remain in the Single Market by some means, will examine these figures for themselves. Then they can explain to the media, to their supporters, and to the rest of us, why they think the British people should have paid the political and economic costs of remaining in the Single Market, or should pay whatever costs might be necessary to maintain some sort of partial membership.

The reasons are not self-evident from figures of export growth over the past 23 years. Perhaps they are concerned about the undoubted inconvenience and increased paperwork, procedures, delays, and therefore costs, for many UK exporters after leaving the Single Market. But many exporters in non-members apparently cope with these hindrances rather well, without them having a noticeable impact on the growth of their exports. Perhaps they fear that UK exporters would not cope so well, and have reason to fear that UK exports would grow even less outside the Single Market than they have inside it. If so, they have to present an argument with evidence and to explain why membership is worth the costs that they want the British people to pay.

6

How have exporters to the EU under WTO rules performed?

The evidence thus far has mainly referred to the difference between member and non-member countries, but the present debate about the best Brexit option is about the type of trading relationship that the UK, as a new non-member, might best try to establish with the EU.

In their attempt to persuade the British people to vote to remain inside the EU, George Osborne and the Treasury identified the three possible kinds of post-Brexit trading relationship with the EU. The first, and most attractive in their view, was what is now called a soft Brexit, in which the UK would remain a member of the EEA like Norway and Iceland. Such a relationship, the Treasury estimated, had boosted the trade of these two countries with the EU by somewhere between 35 and 53 per cent, well short of the 68 to 85 per cent boost from EU membership, but nonetheless the best that could be expected of a non-member.[1] The second was to negotiate bilateral agreements like Switzerland's, which had lifted its trade with the EU, according to the Treasury, by between 14 and 21 per cent. The third relationship, the baseline for all its estimates, was to trade merely under WTO rules, which would provide no boost to UK trade at all. Trading under WTO rules was therefore, in the view of the Treasury, the least attractive post-Brexit option for the UK.

The Treasury's long-term predictions of the losses to UK trade and GDP by 2030, should the UK leave the EU, seem to have been discredited and largely forgotten. However, their estimates of the relative benefits of these three kinds of trade relationship still appear to have some currency in the present debate, and in particular to have persuaded those favouring a soft Brexit.

As mentioned earlier, on the 7th October 2016, the heads of four industrial federations, the CBI, the EEF, the ICC, and techUK, published an open letter to the Prime Minister which said:

> Every credible study that has been conducted has shown that this WTO option would do serious and lasting damage to the UK economy and those of our trading partners. The Government should give certainty to business by immediately ruling this option out under any circumstances.[2]

They did not identify the credible studies they had in mind, but one suspects they had the Treasury analysis in mind. On 18th January 2017, Sir Andrew Cahn, former chief executive of UKTI, cited their analysis, on BBC Radio 4's *Today* programme, to warn of a 7.5 per cent fall in GDP if the UK traded under WTO rules.[3]

If for the sake of the argument, however, we put aside the reasons given above as to why the Treasury analysis is less than credible, we may evaluate it in another way – by comparing the readily accessible past record of exports to the EU, of countries under different trading relationships, over the life of the Single Market. We will, in short, be comparing the actual record of countries with these differing trading relationships with the EU, in which we might expect to find evidence of the varying levels of benefits on which the Treasury based their estimates of each relationship's attractiveness to the UK post-Brexit.

Table 6.1 shows the growth of goods exports to 11 other founder members of the EU Single Market from 22 non-member countries whose exports exceeded $10 billion in 2015.[4] The 22 trading partners are ranked in order of the growth in the value of their exports over the 23 years, and distinguished from one another by the kind of trading relationship they enjoyed with the EU.

Korea is left as trading under WTO rules, even though it concluded a bilateral agreement with the EU which came into force in 2011, since for most of this period it was trading with the EU under WTO rules.

If the Treasury estimates were consistent with past performance, one would expect to find exports between fellow members of the

Table 6.1: Real growth of goods exports to the founder members of the Single Market, 1993-2015

in 4 trade relationships: as fellow members, as EEA members, under bilateral FTAS and under WTO rules in US(1993)$

Partner country	Trading relationship	% Real Growth from 1993 to 2015	Value of Exports ($bn 2015)
Bangladesh	WTO	794	10.0
China & HK	WTO	545	269.1
Russia	WTO	417	108.4
India	WTO	348	31.3
Turkey	Bilateral	277	40.0
Mexico	Bilateral	235	13.1
Morocco	Bilateral	217	11.6
Nigeria	WTO	198	15.7
Total WTO	**WTO**	**135**	**829.5**
Norway	EEA	129	49.7
Total Bilateral	**Bilateral**	**107**	**191.7**
Malaysia	WTO	98	15.7
Brazil	WTO	94	28.4
Korea*	WTO	90	24.2
Switzerland	Bilateral	84	94.5
Thailand	WTO	77	14.9
Algeria	Bilateral	75	19.7
Indonesia	WTO	73	12.1
EU11	**EU**	**70**	**1585.9**
Singapore	WTO	70	22.8
U.S.	WTO	68	197.0
South Africa**	Bilateral	65	12.8
Canada	WTO	54	14.2
Saudi Arabia	WTO	46	18.8
UK	**EU**	**25**	**176.8**
Japan	WTO	-36	46.8

*FTA with EU came into force 2011
**South Africa 1993-97 is EU import Data

Source: IMF DOTS, data.imf.org, accessed 4/11/2016

Single Market at the top of the table, since the Treasury estimated that membership had boosted intra-EU trade by between 68 percent and 85 per cent. Beneath them would come those with the most attractive post-Brexit option of EEA membership, Norway and Iceland, followed by countries with bilateral agreements like Switzerland, and finally, lowest and slowest of all, and therefore at the bottom of the table, would be the exports of those who trade simply as WTO members.

In the event, the recorded export performance of countries with these different trade relationships is almost the opposite of the Treasury estimates. The top of the table is dominated by those trading under WTO rules, supposedly the most disadvantaged and the worst post-Brexit option for the UK. Their aggregate growth is higher than that of the only EEA country in the table.[5] It is also higher than the countries which have bilateral agreements with the EU. Still more surprising is that their exports have grown almost twice as much as the exports of the other eleven founder members of the Single Market to each other, as well as those of the UK, all of which have – according to the Treasury – been boosted by 115 per cent as a result of EU membership.

Thus, according to the CBI, EEF, the ICC, and techUK, the option thatthe Government should be 'immediately ruling out… under any circumstances' is the trading relationship of many of the most successful exporters to the EU over the past 23 years. Perhaps they fear that the UK would end up with the growth of Japan, the only one of the 15 countries trading under WTO rules that ended up with a lower rate of growth than the UK. We can only guess what was in their minds since they declined to identify any of the credible studies that prompted their plea to remain in the Single Market.

This evidence suggests that leaving the Single Market and trading under WTO rules is not as fearsome as these trade associations, along with the cross-party band of MPs and other supporters of soft Brexit, would like us to believe. Of course, it will be inconvenient for exporters, and no one wants UK exporters, or importers for that matter, to face tariff barriers. But, if the UK is obliged to do so as its default option, this evidence does not suggest that it 'would do serious and lasting damage to the UK economy'.

7

A closer look at the impact of EU trade agreements

Table 6.1 does not distinguish between the dates at which the agreements of the six countries identified as having bilateral agreements with the EU came into force. Since their agreements did not all begin in 1993 the figure of their aggregate growth might well be misleading. Some were trading for some of these years under WTO rules, and the overall growth figure might not therefore capture the benefits resulting from their agreements with the EU. A further short analysis was therefore conducted to see whether the exports of these six countries, and four more countries with which the EU has concluded bilateral agreements, as well as the two EEA countries, grew faster than 94 countries trading under WTO rules *after* their agreements with the EU came into force.

The answer is given in Table 7.1. Post-agreement growth in the five shaded countries was faster than that of those trading under WTO rules, but in the other seven it was not. No doubt the post-agreement impact of agreements is worthy of more detailed investigation, and they are examined further in Chapter 17, but this data gives no reason for thinking that the table above has given an altogether misleading impression of the relative advantages of trading under WTO rules.

Table 7.1: Real growth of exports to the single market (EU12)

Two EEA and 10 countries with bilateral agreements vs 94 countries trading under WTO rules in US 1993 dollars

Partner with trade agreement	Trade agreement in force from	% Export growth from year FTA in force to 2015	% Export growth of 94 countries under WTO rules over the same period**
Iceland	1993*	143	127
Norway	1993*	111	127
Switzerland	1993*	85	127
Turkey	1996	203	94
Israel	2000	24	66
Mexico	2000	144	66
Morocco	2000	59	66
South Africa	2000	39	66
Chile	2003	18	65
Egypt	2004	56	39
Algeria	2005	-28	19
Korea	2011	-17	-21

*These countries had agreements with the EU prior to Single Market
**The 94 countries are those without a regional trade agreement with the EU that report their export data to the EU12 countries with the IMF.

Source: IMF Direction of Trade Statistics (accessed at data.imf.org on 06/11/2016)

8

A synoptic view of trading with the EU under four different relationships

After these various selective views on trade in goods with the EU, Table 8.1 attempts to provide a synoptic view of UK exports to the EEC/EU, alongside exports of other members and of countries trading with the EEC/EU under three different relationships over the 43 years of the UK's membership.

The UK is given separately, followed by the EU12, the founding members of the Single Market. Three of them were not members of the EEC in 1973, but they have nonetheless been included so that there is a uniform set of countries to compare over the 43 years. The EEA 2 are Norway and Iceland. The Treasury generalized about the benefits of this relationship but since the population of Norway is more than 15 times Iceland's, and its GDP 23 times larger, it is obviously very high risk to do so, being *de facto* just one case. The same might be said of Bilateral 2, Switzerland and Turkey, as the character of their agreements is utterly different. Turkey's entails membership of the EU Customs Union, while Switzerland's does not. Moreover the Swiss-EU agreements only came into force circa 1990-92, and Turkey's in 1996, so during the years of the Common Market, they might have been classified in the last group, trading under WTO rules. They are, however, two of the longest running EU agreements (though preceded by agreements with Syria in 1973 and Andorra in 1991) and are the best available exemplars of this type of trade relationship. Many other EU bilateral agreements followed at varying intervals after 2000. These cannot, however, be easily added to a single table, and are considered separately later.

The 14 countries trading under WTO rules are Bangladesh, Brazil,

Canada, Hong Kong, India, Indonesia, Japan, Korea,[1] Malaysia, Nigeria, Saudi Arabia, Singapore, Thailand and the U.S. They are all the countries for which data is available in the IMF Direction of Trade database and whose exports to the EU exceeded $10 billion in 2015. This is an arbitrary cut-off point of course, and means a good number of small, emergent countries are excluded. A full set of data is not available for, among others, Australia, China, Russia, and three oil states, Qatar, Bahrain and UAE. However, we are left with a diverse collection of countries, which may well come closer to the EU12, in both trading experience and scale, than the other comparisons.

After excluding China, for whom IMF export data begins only in 1978, it seemed as if a significant piece of the synoptic picture of EU trade was missing. A second row of countries trading under WTO rules, with China added to the original 14, has been included, out of curiosity, and simply to show what difference it would have made over these years to the growth of the WTO trade had a full set of data been available. The missing years were reconstructed by assuming that the growth rate 1973-1977 was the same as that 1978-1982.

The 43 years are shown in four columns, each referring to periods of time that are of interest analytically:

1. The 20 years of the Common Market, 1973-1992

2. 23 years of the Single Market, 1993-2015

3. The pre-crisis Single Market years, 1993-2008

4. Export growth over the entire period of UK membership, 1973-2015.

Since the table compresses a great deal of evidence, each of the four periods is discussed separately overleaf.

Table 8.1: Real growth of goods exports to EU11 by 30 nations according to their trade relationship with the EU in four time periods (1973 US dollars)

Exports of goods to EU 11 by	1. 1973 to 1992		2. 1993 to 2015		3. 1993 to 2008		4. 1973 to 2015	
	% Real Growth	% CAGR	% Real Growth	% CAGR	% Real Growth	% CAGR	% Real Growth	% CAGR
UK	205	6.04	25	1.00	74	3.77	200	2.65
EU 12	125	4.37	64	2.28	132	5.76	199	2.64
EEA 2	184	5.65	133	3.91	296	9.61	463	4.20
Bilateral 2	180	5.57	117	3.58	144	6.11	442	4.10
WTO 14	119	4.22	52	1.93	93	4.47	198	2.63
WTO 15	124	4.34	117	3.59	153	6.39	341	3.60

The two EEA countries are Iceland and Norway, the two with bilateral agreements are Switzerland and Turkey, and the WTO 14 trading only under WTO rules are Bangladesh, Brazil, Canada, Hong Kong, India, Indonesia, Japan, Korea, Malaysia, Nigeria, Saudi Arabia, Singapore, Thailand and the U.S. The WTO 15 is the 14 plus China, and included only of curiosity.

Source: IMF Direction of Trade Statistics (accessed at data.imf.org on 06/11/2016)

1. Export growth under the Common Market decades, 1973-1992

The growth and annual growth rate of the four types of countries during these years depart in one major respect from the estimates of the Treasury. Membership was supposed to be the most favourable relationship for trade with the EEC/EU, but only the UK supports this idea. The EU12 as a whole do not. The growth of the EEA and Bilateral countries is higher, and that of the WTO countries only slightly lower. Suspecting this might be due to the anachronistic inclusion of the three latecomers, Greece, Spain and Portugal, amongst the EU12, it was recalculated without them. Growth of the nine then fell to 118 per cent and their CAGR to 4.19 per cent, and hence were even less consistent with the Treasury estimates than the table shows.

The discrepancy between the UK and the EU12 demonstrates that the Treasury were very unwise to assume that it was possible to generalise from the experience of the EU12 to the UK, and to apply estimates based on EU12 to the UK alone. In a moment, we will see this same discrepancy recurs, though in the opposite direction. It would not be altogether correct, one might add, to attribute the UK's high rate of export growth to EEC membership, since UK exports to these same 11 countries had grown by 137 per cent over the 13 years of EFTA membership preceding entry at the still higher CAGR of 7.45 per cent. Hence, the rate of growth of UK goods exports to member countries did not climb after entry to the EEC. It fell, while nonetheless remaining higher than that of other countries.

The Treasury estimates were, one must add, correct about the other three relationships, in that the EEA countries were ahead of the Bilaterals, if only marginally, and both were well ahead of the WTO countries.

2. Export growth over the Single Market years, 1993-2015

Growth over the Single Market years, in the blue column, shows a remarkable reversal of fortunes for the UK. Having grown fastest under the Common Market, their exports have recorded the slowest growth during the 23 years of the Single Market. They have been far surpassed by those of the EEA countries, by the two Bilaterals, quite markedly by the EU12 collectively, and even by the fourteen countries trading under WTO rules. The Treasury estimated, it will be recalled, that UK trade in goods had, by virtue of EU membership, received a 115 per cent boost compared with these countries. There is little sign of it.

The Treasury model did not merely fail to pick up the UK's remarkable reversal; it actually predicted the exact opposite. An annex of its report observed that

> the EU membership effect is found to be considerably more positive after implementing the 1987 Single Market Act than in the preceding years... the impact of EU membership on goods trade post-1987 is approximately double that of the pre-1987 impact... The lagged dummy variables are all positive which suggests that the trade benefits from EU membership increase over time, suggesting the estimates used may underestimate the overall impact of EU membership.[2]

The IMF figures say the opposite. The CAGR of UK exports was 6.04 per cent over the Common Market decades from 1973 to 1992 and fell to just 1.00 per cent over the Single Market years from 1993 to 2015. Who are we to believe? The IMF data or the lagged dummy variables of the Treasury model? Is this an example of lies, damn lies and statistics? No, not really. There is one critical difference between the two. There is only one person in a thousand who could check the assumptions, guesses, proxies that lie behind the Treasury's dummy variables, whereas everyone who has a computer can check the IMF data, and this presentation of it, with a few clicks.

For the moment, however, we may put aside the UK, and look at the record of the growth of the EU12's exports over these years, since it also contradicts the Treasury model. Counter-intuitive as it may sound, EU membership has not been the most advantageous relationship for exporting to the Single Market over these 23 years. The growth and CAGR of founder members exporting to each other have been comfortably exceeded by the two EEA countries, and by the two countries trading with the help of bilateral agreements. But the founder members did manage to grow more than the countries trading under WTO rules.

One might add, parenthetically, that it is just as well that the Chinese figures were not quite complete. If they had not been excluded, the results would have been still more embarrassing for the Treasury, with the countries trading under WTO rules recording a higher rate of growth of exports to the founder members of the Single Market than the growth of founder members' exports to each other.

3. Export growth under the pre-crisis Single Market years, 1973-2008

The third column of figures shows, not surprisingly, that the financial crisis adversely affected the exports of every country whatever their trade relationship with the EU. The UK seems to have been slightly more affected than the others. The growth of its exports up to the onset of the crisis was three times higher than it eventually proved to be by 2015. However, the more important point to note is that, before the crisis, its growth and growth rate lagged behind those of the 14 WTO countries.

Once again, both the EEA and Bilateral countries have recorded higher rates of growth than the EU12 exports to each other, the latter by a small margin, but the EU12 did record higher growth than the WTO14. The Treasury score another point, as long as China is kept out of the picture.

4. Export growth over 43 years, 1973-2015

The fourth column of figures is simply a summation of the entire 43 years of the UK's EU membership. The UK ends up with growth and a growth rate virtually the same as that of the EU as a whole, a specious resemblance we now know, and most probably the result of the UK's rapid growth over the Common Market years. More strikingly, the growth of both the UK and EU12 over the 43 years has been virtually the same as that of the WTO14, a finding which has significant consequences for Brexit negotiations and policy. The growth of all three – the UK, the EU12 and the WTO14 – is, however, significantly lower than that recorded by the EEA and Bilateral countries, further confirming, if it was needed, that the Treasury estimates are mistaken. The EEA and Bilateral countries also very similar to one another, which is just one more mistaken Treasury estimate.

Interim conclusions about the UK's Brexit options

Any resemblance, one feels bound to say, between the historical reality recorded in these figures, and the predictions about the advantages of various kinds of post-Brexit trade relationship presented by the Treasury to the British people, is purely accidental.[3] Most of these figures contradict the Treasury estimates in one way or another. About the only consistent pattern is that the two EEA and two Bilaterals consistently outperform the others. This is not consistent with the Treasury estimates, since membership of the EU was supposed to be the best option. However, because of the small size of both, it is, as noted at the beginning, risky to draw conclusions about these trading relationships from these results.

Once again, it is lucky for the Treasury that data for China was not included, otherwise the member countries that they thought had the most advantageous trade relationship would have ended up with the lowest export growth of all. After 43 years the UK and the EU have enjoyed an advantage in export growth over this collection of 14 countries trading under WTO rules of one and two percentage points, and of 0.01 and 0.02 percentage points in terms of compound annual growth. These results emphatically vindicate Wolfgang Münchau's verdict of the Single Market as 'a giant non-event'.[4] There is little sign of the 115 per cent boost to the trade in goods that UK and other EU members were supposed to have received as a result of their membership. Incidentally, if it were true that they have been receiving this boost, these results would contradict the gravity theory, since their export growth would have been comfortably exceeded by the 14 countries from around the world trading under WTO rules. Either the Treasury estimate is wrong or the gravity theory on which it is based, or maybe both.

This table does not, of course, take account of any of the costs to those countries who pay for membership of the Single Market. If there was some way of doing this, it seems highly unlikely that continued membership would prove to be the more attractive option.

In the present context, the most pertinent comparison is not the entire 43 years, but that giving the growth and growth rates over the 23 Single Market years. Theresa May has decided not to keep the UK in the Single Market, but her critics think she was mistaken and that a considerable economic cost will be paid for this decision. But these critics receive little support from these figures of goods export growth. The table has shown that the Single Market has coincided with a very poor period for the growth of UK goods exports. They compare unfavourably with every comparator group. The argument for remaining a member of the Single Market and bearing its costs would have to take the form of showing that outside it UK exports to the EU would have grown, or will grow, significantly less.

At first glance, the best UK option would appear to be either bilateral or EEA agreements. However, EEA membership entails obligations which the UK would be unlikely to accept. Further still, generalising from either experience or taking them as a guide to any UK decision would be extremely high risk, given that there are just two cases of each, and *de facto* just one in the case of the EEA. As noted in Appendix I, that generalising from the EU to the UK was one of the Treasury's main errors. This would be several times worse.

Bearing all these reservations in mind, trading under WTO rules remains a promising rival option. A diverse collection of countries, leaving out China, have demonstrated that they have been able to increase their exports to the EU at a rate considerably higher than that of the UK over the past 23 years, despite the tariff and non-tariff barriers they have faced and without the advantages of membership supposedly enjoyed by the UK, including the supposed 115 per cent boost from membership to its goods exports. Certain readily identifiable sectors, notably agriculture, would be hard hit if the UK chose this option, since the prohibitively high agriculture tariffs and the EU's CAP could act as a significant barrier to exports. However, putting agriculture and the few other sectors aside for the moment, these figures clearly show many countries have traded successfully with the Single Market under WTO rules no less successfully than its own members. That being so, there is no reason to dismiss it as a viable Brexit option.

If the record of growth in goods exports during the Single Market offers any guidance for the future, and it is hard to think of a better one, the first lesson is that the UK was well advised to say that it would withdraw from it. The second lesson is the reassuring one that trading under WTO rules is a perfectly acceptable default position. It could hardly be a national disaster or do 'serious and lasting damage to the UK economy', since the exports of many countries trading under these rules have grown at a faster rate than those of the UK. Moreover, as we shall see in a moment, UK exports to countries with which the UK trades under WTO rules have grown faster than UK exports to the EU. If a reasonable trade agreement covering agriculture and other significantly affected sectors can be agreed, then the most significant costs for UK exporters would be the inconvenience of applying procedures they currently use for

56 per cent of their goods exports to the remaining 44 per cent. Damnably annoying, no doubt, but some way short of a national disaster.

We won't do it! The EU view of UK choosing to trade with the EU under WTO rules

Sir Ivan Rogers, former UK Representative to the EU, to the European Scrutiny Committee 1 February 2017:

'I think the view from many [of the EU 27] will be that the implications for the UK of walking away without any deal, on the economic side, without any preferential agreement, and walking into a WTO-only world, are from their perspective, which may be a mis-reading of us, so unpalatable that we won't do it. But I think that will become a major question during 2017.

'… I think the calculation on the other side will be that the UK will see that it's in its interest, in a whole plethora of areas, to have a future preferential deal with the EU, and that that will oblige us to think seriously about transitional arrangements which bridges to that deal. And that a unilateral abrogation or a desire to simply walk away from the table, and say 'well if your sticking liabilities of that sort on the table we're not playing' is not a route that they think we will take.'*

*He was referring to the idea that the EU wished to levy a departure fee on the UK of between 40 and 60 billion euros

9

How has UK fared when exporting under WTO rules?

Some critics of hard Brexit imagine that if the UK were to leave the Single Market and trade with its members under WTO rules it would be 'stepping into the unknown', but that cannot be an accurate description, since the UK currently exports to 111 countries under WTO rules.[1] Its experience of doing so therefore provides a real world reference point, for what might happen if the UK has to accept, or prefers to accept, trading under WTO rules with the 27 members of the EU.

Figure 9.1 gives the latest view from the IMF data. It shows UK exports of goods to three groups of countries: the EU14, meaning all the founder-members plus Austria, Finland and Sweden who joined in 1995; 62 countries or territories with which the EU has trade agreements, from which the UK exports may have benefited; and the 111 countries with which the UK currently trades under WTO rules.[2]

As it happens, UK exports to countries with which it trades under WTO rules have grown at a CAGR of 2.88 per cent which is more rapidly than either the 0.91 per cent to fellow EU members, and the 1.82 per cent to countries with which the EU has concluded trade agreements. According to the Treasury, membership of the EU had boosted UK goods exports by 115 per cent, meanwhile UK exports to countries under WTO rules received no assistance from any kind of trade agreement, making their growth rate still more remarkable.

Yet the argument is still made that, if the UK were to enlarge the number of countries with which it trades under WTO rules, it

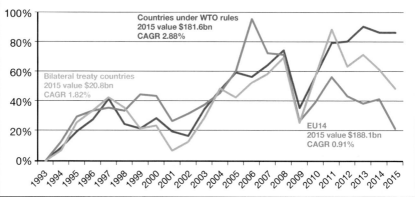

Figure 9.1: Real growth of UK exports of goods, 1993-2015
to the EU14, to 62 countries with which the EU has bilateral treaties
and to 111 countries to which it has exported under WTO rules
[with CAGR calculated using US1993 dollars]

Source: IMF Direction of Trade statistics (accessed at data.imf.org on 06/11/2016)

would do 'serious and lasting damage to the UK economy'. Really? What evidence is there for this assertion? And how would this damage occur? The main problem for UK exports has been the low rate of growth to the EU14 for the past 23 years. Why should the UK negotiate or pay for something that does not appear to have helped its exporters?

10

Scotch versus Bourbon: exports of an EU member and a 'most favoured nation'

The data presented thus far have repeatedly shown that UK exports to fellow members of the Single Market have grown more slowly over its 23 years than those of many non-member countries. Other EU members' exports have generally grown more rapidly than those of the UK, but their growth too has been surpassed by many non-member countries.

This baffling paradox seems to have passed unnoticed. Principally, one suspects, because it has never been the responsibility of the Treasury or of any other department of the UK government, or apparently of anyone else, including the European Commission, to regularly monitor and report on the impact of the Single Market on its members, and to evaluate it by comparison with countries that have not been members of it. Leaders of all the major political parties in the UK have encouraged the British people to think of it as a thoroughly good thing, despite one or two admitted flaws (such as the euro and the Schengen Agreement which can be forgotten as they do not apply to the UK) and despite offering no evidence to support their views. They appear to have had a considerable measure of success and even persuaded many of those who are eurosceptic on other grounds, including many leave voters.[1] Moreover, a good number of UK companies directly engaged in exporting to the Single Market, and many trade associations on behalf of their members, have added their voices to the chorus of approval.[2] Since they are directly involved in exporting to the Single Market, and the rest of us are not, their opinions have to be taken seriously.

It is not, however, easy to do so, since they too have declined to publish evidence in support their views, even when expressly invited to do so by the Foreign and Commonwealth Office (FCO) when it organised the Balance of Competences Review in 2013. The majority of submissions expressed support for the Single Market and the trade agreements of the EU. Support was sometimes qualified, but never accompanied by research that measured benefits, either for their own sectors and member companies or for the UK economy as a whole. None attempted to say whether benefits they enjoyed outweighed the costs for non-exporting UK industries or UK taxpayers. They simply expressed qualified or unqualified support for the EU and the Single Market, and left it at that. A reader is therefore left unable to judge whether they were simply grateful for the convenience of membership. Or, whether the benefits have actually enabled businesses to compete more effectively with non-EU member countries, either in the Single Market itself or around the world, thereby bringing them significant gains in exports, efficiency, profits, investment, growth and employment.

The submission of the Scotch Whisky Association (SWA) to that review was probably the most warmly enthusiastic about the merits of EU membership.[3] Unlike many others, its support for the EU, and the balance of competences at the time was unqualified, and its submission was illustrated with a number of telling examples of how standardized EU regulations had helped the marketing of whisky within the EU, and how the commission had facilitated and defended market access for its members' products around the world. Like the other associations, however, it did not present any hard data about how the industry has benefited from the Single Market or the EU trade agreements which it so warmly commended.

The UN Comtrade database, however, supplies one piece of the missing data. It allows us to see just how much the exports of the whisky industry have benefited from both membership of the Single Market and the trade agreements that the European Commission has negotiated, by giving the value of intra and extra-EU exports of Scotch over the years from 1993 to 2014.

These benefits may, of course, only be judged by comparing

the growth of the exports of its members to the EU with that of a competitor from a non-member country that has to sell to the EU under WTO rules. Bourbon distilled in Kentucky and elsewhere in the Southern U.S. seems as close as we can get to a direct competitor, though that is not especially close, since Bourbon has only begun to be sold internationally in relatively recent decades, whereas Scotch has long been, as the association proudly puts it, 'the world's foremost internationally traded spirit drink'.

In 1993, total sales of Scotch to the other founder members of the Single Market were more than eleven times larger than the total sales of Bourbon to them plus the UK ($1.2 billion versus $105 million), and nearly 15 times larger without the UK ($81 million). However, over the years 1993 to 2014, exports of Scotch to the EU have grown erratically with a real CAGR, in 1993 US$, of -0.77 per cent, while sales of Bourbon have, by contrast, grown steadily and rapidly, with a real CAGR of 5.8 per cent.[4]

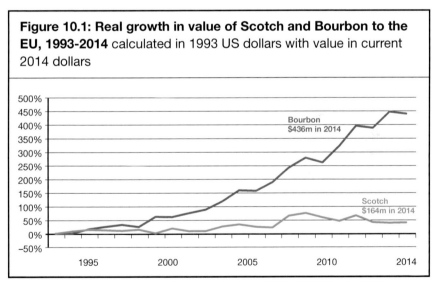

Figure 10.1: Real growth in value of Scotch and Bourbon to the EU, 1993-2014 calculated in 1993 US dollars with value in current 2014 dollars

Source: United Nations Commodity Trade Statistics Database (COMTRADE) HS code 2208.30. www. comtrade.un.org.

As a result, after 22 years enjoying the many benefits of the Single Market, exports of Scotch to the EU had grown by 39.3 per cent, while Bourbon had increased 437.0 per cent, and whereas in 1993 Scotch exports had been nearly 15 times the value of Bourbon, they were less than four times the value in 2014. No doubt, part of the reason for Bourbon's success is that the EU tariff in distilled spirits has been progressively reduced to zero over these years.

Scotch remains ahead in sales to the EU, and by quite a margin, but the Single Market does not appear to have brought any significant comparative advantage over its closest non-member competitor. The SWA plainly enjoys a warm relationship with the European Commission officials, but sitting at the EU tables and helping to make the rules does not appear to have counted for much in the EU marketplace. Not sitting at the table, and not helping to make the rules, does not appear to have troubled Kentucky Bourbon distillers in the slightest.

The association also spoke warmly of the benefits of EU FTAs in wider world markets, as well as the European Commission's defence of its trade interests in them, and did not think the UK acting on its own could possibly replicate this support. In 2013, a comprehensive analysis of the Scotch whisky industry in *The Economist* also took this view and decided, also in the absence of any relevant comparative data, that 'the EU is now the industry's essential sword and shield for conquering world markets'. UN Comtrade allows us to see just how well the industry's 'essential sword and shield' have enabled it to conquer world markets.

Figure 10.2 compares the rate of real growth of Scotch exports in world markets with that of Bourbon from 1993 to 2014. In the first year, 1993, Scotch had far larger world sales, nearly twelve times larger, $3188.5 million versus Bourbon's $274 million. Twenty two years later, with Scotch recording a compound annual growth rate in world sales of 1.2 per cent, and Bourbon a rate of 5.2 per cent, Scotch sales were, at $6.7 billion, just over five times larger than Bourbon's $1.3 billion. Bourbon seems to have performed remarkably well. Despite the EU's sword and shield, Scotch has not been able to keep pace.

What are we to learn from this comparison? Since Bourbon no longer faces any EU tariff we cannot of course draw conclusions about other British industries that would face a tariff if they had to trade under WTO rules post-Brexit. But Bourbon's performance does confirm, once again, what we have seen in many of the preceding tables, that in itself trading under WTO rules does not

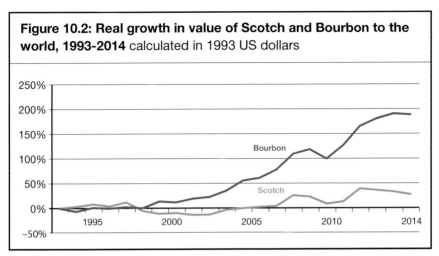

Figure 10.2: Real growth in value of Scotch and Bourbon to the world, 1993-2014 calculated in 1993 US dollars

Source: United Nations Commodity Trade Statistics Database (COMTRADE) HS code 2208.30. www.comtrade.un.org.

preclude rapid growth of exports to the EU. It also suggests that Scotch and other industries that would face zero or minimal tariffs after Brexit have no reason to fear the transition from trading with the EU as a most favoured nation under WTO rules. Inconvenience, yes! A serious impact on the volume and value of their sales, no!

Another lesson is that while trade associations and individual firms may speak strongly in favour of the Single Market and the EU's trade agreements, their testimony should be viewed sceptically, unless accompanied by evidence about the export growth of their products alongside that of non-member competitors.[5] A good working relationship with the European Commission, and help in making and enforcing EU rules, as well as the undoubted current convenience of exporting to fellow members, are not adequate grounds on which the merits of membership of the Single Market, or of alternative Brexit options for the UK, should be judged.

Post-referendum thoughts of the Scotch Whisky Association and others

Having consulted members after the referendum, the Scotch Whisky Association set out the 'consequences, challenges and opportunities' presented by Brexit in a press release on 3rd August 2016 entitled 'Brexit – what now for Scotch Whisky?'[6]

After reading its super-enthusiastic submission to the Balance of Competences Review in 2013, or *The Economist*'s puff, one might have expected that it would insist on continued membership of the Single Market via a soft Brexit. In the event, the SWA's first priority was simply for 'a UK trade policy that is as open and free trading as possible'. The rest of its priorities were entirely manageable concerns about future administrative and customs arrangements and FTAs.

Other Scots voices are much more decided about the need for a soft Brexit than its foremost exporting industry. In early November the Scottish Council for Development and Industry published a paper for the Scottish Parliament. It was guided by a model constructed by NIESR (the Treasury also made use of the NIESR model) from which it learned that 'UK service exports could be cut by 60 per cent and goods exports cut by 35 to 40 per cent if the UK exporters do not have access to the EU single market'. Not surprisingly, it decided that Brexit 'on the same terms as EU membership or as close to them as possible would be in the interests of Scottish exporters', while operating under WTO rules would, it thought, be 'highly detrimental' to the 100 Scottish firms that account for 60 per cent of Scottish exports.[7] In the light of the UN Comtrade data above, this assertion seems more than a little exaggerated. Why should it be highly detrimental to Scotch whisky distillers, if they had to trade under the same terms as Bourbon distillers? Unfortunately, models are quite good at spreading terror, but they can't answer straightforward questions like this.

On 15th November 2016, the Scottish Parliament passed a motion supporting Scotland's continuing membership of the European Single Market. On 20th December 2016, the Scottish Government published a policy statement which purported to show that a hard Brexit would be a 'national disaster' for Scotland.[8] The limited economic evidence and argument in this statement is intertwined with, and obscured by, the political manoeuvring of the Scottish Government. The former is rendered incoherent by the latter. It is examined in detail in Appendix III.

To suggest that 'trading under WTO rules', would be a disaster for Scotland's number one exporter, when Bourbon has been flourishing under them, is offensive and absurd.

11

Strange Brexiteer arguments against trading under WTO rules

Flexcit: A plan for leaving the European Union, by the Leave Alliance, is a thoughtful, carefully argued and copiously documented analysis of the process of leaving the EU, which was first published some months before the referendum.[1] Over its 400 pages, its authors examined every possible option, and every aspect of the Brexit process in some detail. Along with *Change or Go*, the massive analysis by Business for Britain, this work gives the lie to Remainers who claimed that no Brexiteers had any idea or plan of what to do if they won the referendum.

Flexcit looked to secure a smooth, reasonably quick and economically neutral Brexit, and thought that this might best be done by the UK re-joining EFTA and thereby retaining membership of the EEA and the Single Market. For some unexplained reason, it assumed that the referendum could only be won on the grounds that the UK would remain a member of the Single Market, and therefore decided that the UK should accept free movement, subjection to EU rules and continued UK contributions to the EU budget. Since the referendum was not won on these grounds, and virtually all leaders of the Leave campaign made perfectly clear they wanted and expected the UK to leave the Single Market, its argument has naturally lost momentum.

Unfortunately, it lost still more by failing to question its own starting assumption that the Single Market has been of very great benefit to the UK economy. It provides one of the striking examples of the way eurosceptics, in this case arch-eurosceptics and dedicated researchers, have been persuaded of the merits of the Single Market without collecting or reviewing any evidence at all. In this respect, they are as one with Messrs Cameron and Osborne and most other ardent Remain campaigners.

However, even though the authors' preferred option of remaining in the Single Market is now off the table, their research on the minutiae of export procedures is still relevant since it amounts to a strong argument in favour of leaving the EU with a trade agreement rather than leaving without one and trading under WTO rules. For them such an option would be disastrous. Their argument may be summarised as follows.

Manufactured goods exported to the EU can only be placed on the market if they meet all the applicable requirements, meaning they have 'undergone the appropriate conformity assessment procedures certified by testing bodies which have been approved by the EU or by systems in originating countries where domestic systems are recognised, usually in conjunction with the international standards body ISO'. EU recognition of exporting countries' conformity assessment is either built into free trade agreements or determined by *ad hoc* mutual recognition agreements (MRAs). Currently, Australia, Canada, Japan, New Zealand, the USA, Israel and Switzerland have MRAs with the EU. China also formalised one in 2014, but it is not yet in force.'

Without the benefit of such agreements and working exclusively under WTO rules, the UK would not have conformity assessment verification in place and would therefore 'have considerable difficulty in securing uninterrupted trade flows.' UK exporters without valid certification documentation will be refused entry, incur very high costs and highly damaging delays and as 'European ports buckled under the unexpected burden of thousands of inspections and a backlog of testing, a huge range of loads would build up while test results and clearance was awaited. The system would grind to a halt. It would not just slow down. It would stop. As has been seen with Channel port disruptions in the past, trucks waiting to cross the Channel would be backed up the motorways nearly to London.'

This last passage seems more than a trifle far-fetched, since there is no reason to think that after a hard Brexit UK exporters will suddenly insist on sending goods to the EU without valid documentation. The earlier passages, however, make a perfectly reasonable, though hardly controversial case, that the UK should negotiate MRAs on conformity assessment with the EU, and with countries with which the EU has trade agreements and MRAs. This case only needs making, however, against the tiny minority who relish an extra hard Brexit in which the UK does not bother to secure any agreements with the EU at all, and decides overnight to abandon its existing EU conformity assessment procedures. The government is hardly likely to choose that course. MRAs on conformity assessment with third countries will, in fact, be much the easiest part of any negotiations, since they will only confirm existing arrangements. Why would countries within and beyond the EU want to disturb the flow of their exports to the UK by not reciprocating?

If the *Flexcit* authors had really hoped to make a convincing case against trading with the EU under WTO rules, they should have examined the countries that have been doing just that over the 23 years of the Single Market, as we have in previous chapters, and then explain why the UK could not be expected to do as well. They might also have spoken to UK exporters who already export around the world under WTO rules, already meeting conformity assessment procedures and facing tariff and non-tariff barriers, and tried to understand why they have managed nonetheless to grow at a faster rate than those who export to the EU. Their fears are entirely imaginary.

Christopher Booker has recently sought to lend support to the Flexcit argument on slightly different grounds, but in a still more hysterical tone. In his column in *The Daily Telegraph* he argued that:

> … leaving it [the Single Market] would be far more disastrous than is generally realised, because one of the countless technicalities to which the lunatic fringe [by which he seems to mean those who wish to leave the Single Market] are oblivious is that in recent years there has been a revolution in the way international trade is organised.
>
> Since the major disruption to trade caused by 9/11, a wholly new system has been emerging, under the auspices of the World Customs Organisation, designed both to improve security and to facilitate

global trade. To prevent crippling delays, cross-border traders sign up to become 'Authorised Economic Operators' (AEOs). This enables them among other things to file all their necessary documentation electronically in advance. It also allows for 'mutual recognition' between customs authorities, so that goods can simply be waved through at their destinations, instead of causing 20-mile tailbacks while they are inspected. But Britain is only part of this global system by virtue of its membership of the EU...

To negotiate separate AEO status in our own right would take far too long; which is why, yet again, by far the simplest and most practical solution is that we should remain, along with Norway and other non-EU countries, in the wider European Economic Area (EEA), thus allowing our AEO status to continue. On the other hand, catastrophically, if we drop out of the single market and lose access to the AEO system, this could strike a devastating blow not just at our trade with the EU but with the rest of the world as well.[2]

Booker seems to have confused and frightened himself in this account of the AEO system. It is, as he correctly observed, organised under the auspices of the World Customs Organisation (WCO). In the UK it is administered by the HMRC which accredits manufacturers, exporters and importers, freight forwarders, warehouse keepers, customs agents, carriers and all those regularly engaged in intra- or extra-EU international trade who meet certain standards of efficiency, security and credit worthiness.[3] While he is correct to say that the UK currently participates as a member of the EU, this is only because member countries operate under same EU laws and treaties, and apply, or try to apply, uniform standards to applicants. They therefore do not need MRAs with each other. According to the WCO compendium of 2016, 41 independent countries also administer AEO programmes, sometimes under different names, to accredit applicants in their own countries. Another 16 are ready to be launched, and 30 more currently under negotiation.[4] Twenty-five of these countries have MRAs, under which they recognise their partner country's AEOs, and grant them privileges equivalent or comparable to their own.

It is absurdly over-blown to suggest, as Booker does, that 'if we drop out of the single market and lose access to the AEO system' it would strike 'a devastating blow not just at our trade with the EU but with the rest of the world as well', and that to obtain 'separate AEO status in our own right would take far too long', and that the UK could therefore only avoid catastrophe by remaining in the EEA. It is almost as if he decided to enter as a late runner in Project Fear.

The 'AEO system' is not in the European Commission's gift and its involvement in it is a legal formality. The system depends on mutual worldwide, cross-country recognition, and it is difficult to see how the UK could 'lose access' to it, since AEO accreditation procedures are currently operated in the UK by HMRC. Why would the EU, or any other country, suddenly decide that the EU and WCO standards the HMRC currently applies are no longer acceptable? Why would the WCO object? It is currently doing its utmost to make the system worldwide. The UK will certainly have to negotiate the re-wording of the seven MRAs of the EU has with other countries, but why should this take long? Full-blown MRA negotiations from scratch have been rapidly agreed. Since the first such agreement in 2007, the US has negotiated 10 MRAs, and is currently negotiating another four. Korea has concluded 10 since 2010, and also has four under negotiation.

Far from being an obstacle to UK trade after a hard Brexit, as Booker seems to imagine, AEOs will facilitate it, and prevent the nightmare scenarios dreamt up by the Flexcit authors from ever occurring. Indeed, one imagines the Department of International Trade will soon seek to minimise the inconvenience to companies involved in post-Brexit intra-EU supply chains, especially if they involve tariffs, by encouraging them all to acquire AEO status as soon as possible. It might well launch an advertising campaign to encourage all UK companies trading with the rest of the world, including SMEs, to be prepared and do the same.[5] It would also be sensible if it drafted MRAs for the 13 countries that have already concluded them with major trading countries, like the US and Japan, but not yet with the EU.

These strange Brexiteer arguments that the UK will be unable to negotiate MRAs on conformity assessments or that its AEOs will not be recognised are fantasies written as if the UK had never traded under WTO rules. It currently does so, with 111 countries.[6]

12

Does a single market in services exist?

Thus far we have been concerned with the export of goods. We will now turn to services. We begin with a simple question that may seem both unnecessary and impolite, since political leaders and commentators have been talking about 'the single market in services' for some years now, does a single market in services actually exist?

The European Commission has a Directorate-General whose business it is to organise and administer this market, seeing that directives are transposed and enforced every year, making grants to those involved in it, publishing action plans, organising networks of consumer centres, updating its website, and so forth. After completing his pre-referendum negotiations, David Cameron announced that one of the reforms he had agreed with other member countries was to 'deepen' the single market in services. George Osborne, with the help of the Treasury, then declared that these improvements to the Single Market would increase UK GDP by two per cent.

The Scottish Government recently expressed its determined opposition to leaving this single market in services since 'our increasingly important services sector is extremely vulnerable to negative effects that are likely to arise if Scotland is required to exit the European Single Market... no trading arrangement in the world offers the degree of access for providers of services that is in any way comparable to that available to members of the European Single Market.'

Is it possible that all these well-informed and powerful persons have been talking about something that does not exist? Impolite or not, one must persist with the question, because by some measures its existence is in doubt, and one would not want those distressed by Mrs May's decision to withdraw from the Single Market to waste their grief on something that does not exist.

The European Commission's favoured index for measuring the single market in services is the relative values of intra- and extra-EU exports as a proportion of EU GDP, a higher proportion of intra-EU exports being taken to show a higher degree of market integration, and therefore the greater the presence of a single market.

The early use of this index by the European Commission suggested that it was just emerging, but little more.[1] The commission however declined, for some reason, to publish regular time series and updates of its growth.[2] One study, using the index, suggested that it had reached a peak in 2007 when intra-EU exports of the EU12 touched 5.98 per cent of their GDP and extra-EU were only 4.87 per cent. From that year on to 2012, however, it appeared to be in decline. In all these countries (except France) extra-EU exports were growing faster than intra-EU exports, and it looked as if evidence of a single market in services might disappear altogether.[3]

The 2015 figures of the EU28 show that it has not done so. Their total intra-EU services exports were valued at $1120.4 billion and were slightly larger than their extra-EU services exports of $940.7 billion, which are respectively 6.90 per cent and 5.80 per cent of EU GDP in 2015, some $16.2 trillion.[4] The 1.10 percentage point difference between the two remains slightly below the 2007 peak, so one has to conclude that while it is not growing steadily or continuously, some element of the single market in services has survived – just about – though clearly it is far larger in politicians' imaginations than it is in reality. The corresponding percentages of EU GDP for goods exports are 20.9 per cent and 12.0 per cent.

There is also evidence on the ground that the promises and chatter about this single market in services run far ahead of the reality. In 2015, the New City Initiative, a trade group of boutique fund managers in the City of London 'conducted exploratory research to discover how 'the "free market" of Europe was working for the asset and wealth management industry'. They were 'amazed to discover that there is no "free market" for financial services'. After giving examples of the costs and national barriers that prevent the free movement of capital, their chairman came to the view: 'If the UK left the EU [assuming trade treaties and other issues can still be negotiated], I do not believe that it would make any difference at all to the ease – or difficulty – of trade for our industry in the EU.'[5]

In their submissions to the Balance of Competences Review, chemical engineers said that though their business was global, the Single Market was a no-go area. Art dealers were also left wondering about the single market's existence, though they were in no doubt about the costs of the regulation it entailed.[6] The British Association of Professional Financial Advisers and the Building Societies Association similarly have complained that while not benefiting from the single market in services in any way, they are obliged to conform to EU directives.[7]

The trade commission of the Legatum Institute opened the first of its informative and detailed briefings on Brexit and financial services in September 2016 with the words: 'Myth 1. There is a single market in financial services, and the only way to have access to it is to be a member of the European Economic Area.' After giving examples, it went on to say 'Access to the single European market is therefore a relatively meaningless term with respect to financial services.' It concluded by suggesting that bilateral Brexit negotiations might well, in what would surely be the supreme irony of the entire Brexit process, contribute towards to the construction of a single EU financial market.[8]

Other measures lead one to be sceptical about the existence of the single market in services. The Services Trade Restrictiveness Index (STRI) of OECD provides profiles indicating the level of access to services markets in different countries. If there was a single market in services, one would expect members to have eliminated the barriers for each other's exporters, and to present a single set of barriers to third country exporters. Neither inference is correct. The STRI profiles of member countries differ widely.[9]

The wide variety of non-tariff barriers that different members of the Single Market present to third countries was demonstrated in the opening offer of the EU in TiSA (Trade in Services Agreements) talks in Geneva in 2013. These were intended to set universal rules for services trade, and for future trade agreements. Twenty-three countries participated along with the EU. However, the 'opening offer' of the EU showed that it did not speak for a Single Market at all, since its 28 members had their own distinctive profile of 'reservations' as illustrated in Figure 12.1.

The lower part of each column shows common EU conditions (members each have some individual exceptions or qualifications to these so they vary by country), and on top of these, the reserved rights or conditions that are specific to each country. On many occasions, of course, groups of EU countries reserve the same rights, but at the end of the day all 28 members have their own unique profile of national reservations. Since the EU has to negotiate on all members behalf, the EU cumulative column of reservations on the left hand side soars above those of the members.

The three columns on the far right of Figure 12.1 show the reserved rights of three non-EU members of the Single Market which have been added, because they also have published their opening offers. Their reserved rights are all lower than those of all EU members, and are all of course national ones. However, for the sake of comparison, those that are roughly similar to the common EU conditions are distinguished from the others in a darker blue.

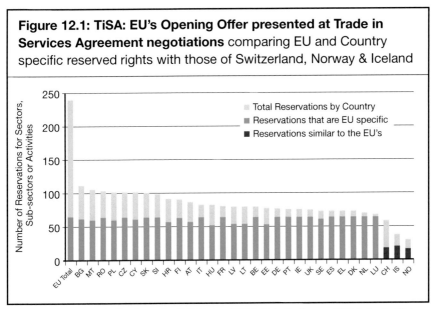

Figure 12.1: TiSA: EU's Opening Offer presented at Trade in Services Agreement negotiations comparing EU and Country specific reserved rights with those of Switzerland, Norway & Iceland

Sources: EU – TiSA Initial offer, September 2013; Swiss – TiSA Initial offer, January 2014; Iceland – TiSA Initial offer, December 2013; Norway – TiSA Initial offer, November 2013. Graphic by Justin Protts, Civitas

These reserved rights were, by the way, repeated in the CETA agreement, so when it comes into force Canadian services exporters and investors will be good informants about whether or not there is a single market in services.[10]

13

Top 40 fastest-growing service exporters to the EU28

Earlier we ranked the top 40 fastest growing significant exporters of goods to the EU founder members of the Single Market and found that, if placed amongst them, the UK would have finished in 36th position. In Table 13.1 we perform a similar exercise with regard to services exports, though it is more difficult to do so. The data is limited to just five years, because the OECD amended the basis of its services data from EBOPS 2002 to EBOPS 2010 and there is therefore no continuous series from an earlier date.[1] The list only includes the larger services exporters, those whose exports to the EU exceeded $2.0 billion in 2014.

The UK has therefore enjoyed rather more success, in terms of the growth of its services exports to other members than of its goods, finishing in 25th place, and the EU 28 finished just above it in 24th.[2]

Like the top 40 goods exporters, they are a heterogeneous collection of small and large, established and emergent economies. Though, since their growth rates refer to only five years, have to be treated cautiously. However, this table serves a similar useful purpose as the earlier top 40, in that it casts serious doubt on the notion that the single market in services has promoted rapid growth of services exports amongst its members while putting non-members at a disadvantage.

Since the single market in services has not promoted more rapid growth of services exports amongst its members, nor put non-members at any noticeable disadvantage, it is difficult to see what the UK will lose by withdrawing from it, or why anyone should be in the least distressed that it has decided to do so. However, since

Table 13.1 Top 40 fastest growing services exporters to the EU, 2010 to 2014

*has trade agreement with the EU which includes services

Exporter		Value in 2014 in US$bn	Growth CAGR
1	Bahamas*	14.0	115.4%
2	Cayman Islands	6.6	35.4%
3	Jersey	9.2	31.2%
4	Guernsey	2.4	26.9%
5	Gibraltar	2.4	25.6%
6	Colombia*	2.5	18.0%
7	Singapore	20.9	11.9%
8	Norway*	20.6	9.1%
9	Panama*	2.2	8.9%
10	Bermuda	28.8	8.9%
11	Vietnam	2.4	8.8%
12	Switzerland*	84.7	8.4%
13	Saudi Arabia	3.6	8.1%
14	United States	252.7	7.6%
15	China	30.4	7.4%
16	UAE	12.8	6.7%
17	Algeria	2.4	6.4%
18	Israel	5.4	6.4%
19	Brazil	10.0	5.9%
20	Korea*	7.9	5.9%
21	Indonesia	2.5	5.6%
22	Chinese Taipei	4.0	5.4%
23	Hong Kong	14.3	5.4%
24	EU28	1,103.3	5.4%
25	United Kingdom	160.0	4.9%
26	Serbia	2.4	4.8%
27	Malaysia	4.3	3.8%
28	Mexico	5.1	3.7%
29	Thailand	7.7	3.5%
30	Chile*	2.3	3.4%
31	Morocco	6.8	3.4%
32	Canada	15.1	3.3%
33	Turkey	20.9	2.4%
34	Philippines	2.5	1.9%
35	Japan	20.2	1.8%
36	Australia	10.4	1.4%
37	Russia	16.5	1.1%
38	India	16.0	0.8%
39	Ukraine	3.5	0.4%
40	South Africa	5.9	0.4%

Source: OECD EBOPS 2010 (accessed at stats.oecd.org on 15/12/2016)

we have already warned that growth rates drawn from this limited number of years are risky, we will consider some other evidence that refers to the same question.

14

Members or non-members, who benefits most from the single market in services?

Table 14.1 takes a closer look at all the countries from which the EU imported services with a value of at least $2 billion in value in 2012. The data covers the years from 2004 to 2012 and is drawn from the earlier OECD EBOPS 2002 series to give a longer time span of growth.

In total, there are 54, 27 of them EU members and 27 non-members. They are ranked in order of the compound annual growth rate (CAGR) of their exports over the nine years, though the EU members can, of course, export only to the other 26, while the non-members export to all 27, so they are not perfect matches. The value of each country's exports is also given. EU members are shaded.

If it were true that the Single Market had benefited the services exports of its members to each other, we would expect the shaded member countries to figure disproportionately among the high growth exporters at the top of the ranking, and therefore to be disproportionately on the left hand side of the table.

A slight tendency in that direction is visible, in that the top left quadrant of the table is more shaded than the top right quadrant, though it is also worth noting that, with the exception of Ireland, they are all 2004 entrants or later. Whereas nine of the 12 EU members on the right hand side are founder members of the Single Market, and include all the larger EU economies – Germany, the UK, Italy, France and Spain – alongside Austria and Finland which entered the Single Market in 1995. Norway, the only non-EU member of

Table 14.1: Growth of service exports of 27 EU member & 27 non-member countries to 27 countries of the Single Market, 2004 to 2012

Partner	CAGR % (2004 US$)	2012 value (2012 US$bn)	Partner	CAGR % (2004 US$)	2012 value (2012 US$bn)
Lithuania	14.89	3.32	Finland	4.78	11.40
China	11.01	25.62	Hong Kong	4.42	11.25
Slovakia	10.93	8.29	Israel	4.20	4.30
India	10.51	13.79	Thailand	3.81	6.90
Estonia	9.96	3.06	Australia	3.72	10.42
Ireland	9.85	42.69	Germany	3.65	140.56
Singapore	9.26	15.57	Denmark	3.10	20.44
Romania	9.07	7.18	Canada	2.81	13.10
Luxembourg	8.89	32.77	Chinese Taipei	2.79	3.78
Poland	8.87	22.78	Japan	2.61	20.01
Bulgaria	8.21	4.81	Korea*	2.57	6.05
Latvia	7.35	2.35	Turkey	2.45	18.35
Chile*	6.45	2.10	United Kingdom	2.33	138.97
Argentina	6.36	2.95	United States	2.10	193.68
Slovenia	6.32	3.55	Morocco	1.99	5.10
Russia	6.12	19.39	Egypt	1.49	7.23
Malaysia	6.07	3.71	Belgium	1.44	46.40
Brazil	5.84	8.17	Portugal	1.35	12.94
Malta	5.81	3.58	Italy	1.31	58.88
Netherlands	5.74	91.53	Norway*	1.16	15.78
Czech Rep.	5.73	15.64	Cyprus	1.03	6.83
Hungary	5.65	10.95	Austria	1.00	36.37
Switzerland*	5.60	78.07	France	0.85	101.52
Sweden	5.50	29.88	Spain	0.35	66.20
Nigeria	5.30	2.51	Mexico*	0.07	4.17
Indonesia	5.25	2.44	South Africa	-0.18	5.88
Croatia**	4.88	7.69	Greece	-2.17	16.65

*Indicates countries with which the EU had a trade agreement in force which include services at some point in these years

**Became a member of the EU in 2014

Source: OECD Dataset: EBOPS 2002 - Trade in Services by Partner Country European Union (27 countries) Total Services Imports. 2012 was the final year of the EBOPS 2002 series

the Single Market included, sits among the other founding EU members with relatively low growth in service exports.

If we look at the EU27 in total, their service exports to each other have a CAGR of 3.2 per cent, half a percentage point below the 3.7 per cent weighted CAGR for the non-EU members in the table. This remarkable finding is, one might add, despite the fact that EU countries enjoy an advantage over non-members that is commonly thought to be a decisive determinant of trade growth, an advantage which has absolutely nothing to do with the Single Market: geographical propinquity.

Once again, it has proved difficult to identify the advantages of membership. In terms of exports growth, members do not appear to have gained from 'sitting at the table and helping to make the rules', from their substantial annual contributions, or from accepting free movement of people and other limitations of their sovereignty. And there is no clear evidence that non-members have lost anything by being scattered round the world, or from the non-tariff barriers of the EU.

On the basis of these figures, it is difficult to see why UK services exporters should be particularly bothered by having to leave the Single Market. But these figures evidently do not tell the whole story, since spokespeople of the City of London point to a tangible benefit of the Single Market which would be lost after Brexit. We discuss this later. However, before considering this benefit we will look more closely at Swiss services exports to the EU, since they are often thought to have suffered by being outside the Single Market.

15

Have Swiss services exports suffered outside the Single Market?

Many UK observers, including the Treasury, have taken the view that Switzerland's bilateral agreements with the EU provide limited guaranteed access to trade in services, and, in the words of the Treasury, 'place significant constraints on Switzerland's capacity to export to the EU'. They described these constraints in great, almost loving, detail, presumably to emphasise the disadvantages of non-membership of the EU.[1] The heads of the CBI and other trade associations seem to share this view, and for this reason favoured a soft Brexit which would preserve Single Market membership and make Swiss-style bilateral agreements unnecessary.

The Treasury did not, however, bother to measure these 'significant constraints on Switzerland's capacity to export to the EU'. Although Switzerland does not publish detailed data on its services exports by partner country or with sector breakdowns, they can be put together from the record of EU services imports from Switzerland.

Figure 15.1 shows the real growth of Swiss services exports to the EU over the 16 years from 1999 to 2014 is compared with that of the UK exports, to which both the total and per capita value of the exports of both countries to the EU in 2015 have been added, as well as the real compound annual growth rate.

Despite the disadvantages of being outside the Single Market, having to rely on their limited bilateral agreements, being under all manner of constraints, and having a super-valued franc, Swiss total services exports to the EU have grown, in real terms, by virtually the same amount and at the same rates, as those of the UK over

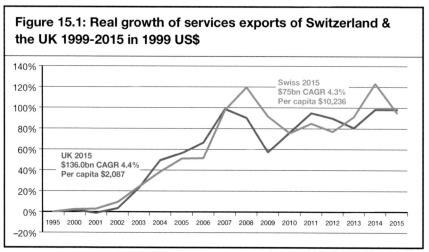

Figure 15.1: Real growth of services exports of Switzerland & the UK 1999-2015 in 1999 US$

Note: Swiss figures are EU15 imports from Switzerland 1999-2003, EU27 imports 2004-2009, and EU28 imports 2010-2015. UK figures are UK exports to EU 26 from 1999-2009, (even though 12 were prospective members for the early years) and to EU 27 2010-2015. Both countries are reported in Extended Balance of Payments for Services (EBOPS) 2002 categories 1999-2009, and in EBOPS 2010 categories 2010-2015 Source: OECD Dataset Trade in Services by partner Country, extracted 12 Feb 2017.

these 16 years. Moreover, in 2015 Swiss service exports were, per capita, almost five times larger than those of the UK. Yet again, the disadvantages of non-membership of the Single Market are difficult to discern.

There is no breakdown of these figures by sector, so it is not possible to say how far Swiss financial services have been handicapped by having limited access to the EU, and how far their superior performance depends on other services. However, current data shows that the financial services exports of the two countries, as a proportion of their total services exports, are virtually the same, about one fifth in both cases, the Swiss slightly less and the UK slightly more.[2] It therefore seems unlikely that the Swiss have been at a vast disadvantage.

16

The big 'known unknown': passports, clearing and other financial services

Although the benefits of the single market in services do not emerge in cross-national comparisons of total services trade, and the Swiss do not appear to have suffered much outside the Single Market, those worried about the consequences of a hard Brexit for financial services can point to one concrete benefit of the Single Market for UK banks – 'passporting'. The passports gained through membership of the Single Market enable banks to be located and regulated in the City of London and under one or other of eight EU directives, to conduct business in any of the other 27 member countries without further authorization from their regulatory authorities.[1]

Further to this, commentators point to the issue of clearing. Clearing of euro-denominated financial instruments is sometimes treated as if it were also a benefit of the Single Market, a facility granted to London by virtue of EU membership which could be withdrawn on leaving the Single Market. François Hollande recently hoped it would be: 'The City, which thanks to the EU, was able to handle clearing operations for the eurozone, will not be able to do them… It can serve as an example for those who seek the end of Europe…? It can serve as a lesson.'

This view of clearing however is somewhat misleading. The only reason that 70 per cent of euro-denominated derivatives are cleared in London is because investors preferred that it be done there rather than anywhere else. Other investors prefer that their dollar and yen and renminbi-denominated instruments are also cleared in London, and some for that matter prefer that their sterling-denominated instruments be cleared in Paris or Frankfurt or Hong

Kong. Governments generally have not worried that instruments denominated in their currency are cleared outside their borders. If the EU should become the first to do so, then clearing euro-denominated financial instruments in London would also be at risk.[2] But that would be because it has decided to erect a barrier against the UK as it left, rather than because it was an inherent feature of the Single Market which the UK had decided to leave.

There is some disagreement about the scale of the impact that the loss of passporting and clearing would cause following Brexit, or indeed whether there would be any losses would at all. They remain, for the moment, a big known unknown.

Estimates of financial services sub-sectors at risk

Attempts are, however, now being made to measure the UK financial services that depend on the EU and are at risk from Brexit. Work on this published so far still seems like hurried initial estimates which will be updated and become increasingly precise and accurate in coming months.

Table 16.1 presents estimates drawn from a recent report by Oliver Wyman (OW) and commissioned by TheCityUK, supplemented by estimates of the financial services at risk post-Brexit in research by Open Europe (OE), on the scale of and likely impact of Brexit on passporting.[3] Both reports gave estimates with ranges of 10 per cent or so, but simply for clarity's sake this table gives only the midpoints of their estimates, which is why some of the percentages do not round to 100.

It divides financial services into three main sectors, with a fourth incorporating the multiplicity of legal, accounting, IT, clearing and other services on which the financial services depend, known as the market infrastructure or ecosystem. It shows the total revenue generated by each sector, and then the proportion of each that is derived from EU-related clients (shaded) alongside the share derived from the rest of the world, and from UK domestic clients alone.

The bottom line estimate is that, in 2015, 22.7 per cent of the revenues of the City of London are EU-related. However, one cannot simply take this 22.7 per cent of total revenue (£45.0 billion)

Table 16.1 Estimates of UK financial services by sector, client location and at risk, 2014/2015

Sector	Total Revenue		Clients Location and Revenue			Estimates of % using passports and therefore at risk
	£bn	as % of all	Location	£bn	as % sector	
Banking	112.5	57	EU	25	22.2	£11.3bn = 45% of £25bn at risk (OW)
			International	22.5	20.0	
			UK	67.5	60.0	
Asset management	21.5	11	EU	5.5	25.6	£3.2bn = 7% 'of total funds under management' (OE)
			International	16.50	38.4	
			UK		38.4	
Insurance	40.5	20	EU	4 (+2.9*)	9.9 (+11*)	£nil - though 3% of Lloyds' GWP make use of passport. (OE)
			International	8.5	21.0	
			UK	28	69.1	
Market Infra (inc clearing)	24	12	EU	10.5	43.8	
			International	14	29.2	
			UK		29.2	
Total	197.50		Total EU	45.0	22.7	

*meaning £2.9bn or 11% of Lloyds' gross written premium (GWP)

Sources: Oliver Wyman, Sept, 2016; Open Europe, Oct 2016, op.cit

as being at risk, or the worst-case post-Brexit loss, because asset management, insurance and pensions, which are EU-related, make little use of passporting.[4]

Passports are less useful for asset managers because the marketing of funds is still subject to a great many national regulations, and hence they often prefer to use subsidiaries for their EU clients. Insurance also relies overwhelmingly on subsidiaries, 87 per cent of its EU business is handled by them and only 13 per cent by passports and branches. Open Europe quotes the CEO of Aviva as saying: 'In the EU there is not one single market. It's no easier for me to do business in France than Singapore or China.'[5] If one is looking for the worst possible case, it is probably better to focus on the EU-related £25 billion of banking services, 45 per cent of which Oliver Wyman thinks is at risk. This means a final figure of £11-12 billion in revenue, to which must be added the lesser known and difficult to estimate proportion of infrastructure services which depend on these EU-related services, and might relocate to the EU if that part of their business could only be conducted there.

Table 16.2 is drawn from ITC services trade data and therefore gives another take on the financial services at risk, but with hard data rather than estimates.[6] Though unfortunately they do not match OW's subsector breakdown, the figures confirm that financial services, though not the largest export sector of UK services to the world in 2014, was the largest UK exporter to the EU, with a quarter of the total, which was by far the largest contribution to the trade balance of the UK.

Table 16.2: UK services exports by sector, destination and trade balance in 2014 (£ billion)

Sector	to world £bn	As % of UK service exports	Trade balance £bn	to EU £bn	As % of services exports to EU	EU as % of UK service exports by sector	Trade balance with EU £bn
All services	221.7	100	89.9	82.0	100.0	37.0	17.3
Manufacturing, maintenance & repair	4.4	0.2	3.3	n/a	n/a	n/a	n/a
Transport	26.9	12.1	7.4	12.0	14.6	44.6	1.5
Travel (inc. education)	28.6	12.7	-10.1	12.2	14.9	42.7	-10.4
Construction	1.99	0.1	0.2	0.73	0.9	36.7	1.1
Insurance & pension	20.3	9.2	18.9	2.5	3.0	12.3	1.9
Financial services	49.7	22.4	39.6	20.4	24.9	41.0	16.7
Intellectual property	11.0	5.2	5.1	4.2	5.1	38.2	2.2
Telecom, information & computer	16.5	7.8	6.98	7.6	9.3	46.1	2.1
Other business services	57.7	27.2	21.8	18.5	22.6	32.1	3.1
Personal, cultural & recreational	2.1	1.0	-1.0	0.72	100.0	34.3	-0.4

Source: ITC Trade Map http://www.trademap.org/

The table provides independent corroboration of the OW estimate of the proportions of financial services that are EU and non-EU related, since it shows that 41.0 per cent of UK financial services exports are to EU28 countries, which is close to the 40:60 split between EU-related and international business in the OW estimates. The City of London Corporation's estimate in 2013 was slightly lower. It thought that 37 per cent of the financial services trade surplus depended on trade with the EU.[7]

These figures are also a reminder of what is often overlooked in the discussion of potential losses that might be incurred by withdrawal from the Single Market, that there is a trade relationship in financial services with the EU. It is not a one-way street. According to the ITC the EU exported financial services to the UK worth £10.1 billion in 2014, so whatever measures might be devised by the EU, either to punish the UK electorate or to attract UK financial services to relocate in the EU, will presumably not wish to disturb the existing EU exporters of financial services to the UK.[8]

The pity is that cross-national data of exports by sub-sectors of financial services is not currently available, since there is little doubt that it would make estimates of the financial services at risk post-Brexit far more accurate. The Swiss figures would be invaluable, but so would those of the US. UK and US exports of financial services are remarkably similar, as the Table 16.3 shows, in total value, in the proportion going to the EU, and in their trade balances on the two bottom lines.

Table 16.3: UK and US services exports by sector, destination and trade balance in 2014 (£ Billion)

	to world in £bn	as % of world service exports	to EU in £bn	EU % of exports by sector	Trade balance with world £bn	Trade balance with EU £bn
All services UK	221.7	100	82.0	38.7	89.9	17.3
All services US	431.1	100	133.0	30.8	141.5	30.7
Insurance & pension UK	20.3	0.9	2.5	12.3	18.9	1.9
Insurance & pension US	10.6	0.24	2.1	19.8	-19.8	-5
Financial services UK	49.7	9.6	20.4	39.7	39.6	16.7
Financial services US	53.0	12.3	20.8	39.2	41.1	15.1

Source: ITC Trade Map http://www.trademap.org/

A breakdown of the kinds of financial services the US exports would be a good indication of the UK sectors that would be unaffected by Brexit. Similar lessons might also be drawn from Hong Kong for, though its total financial services exports to the EU in 2014 were only £2.9 billion, they too might show the type of services that are unaffected by Single Market membership.

The OW estimates conclude with global rather than sub-sector estimates covering a spectrum of Brexit scenarios, which provide high and low access to the Single Market. The two ends of the spectrum are summarized in Table 16.4. The high access end entails retaining 'the same level of access to international markets, and recognised equivalence with non-EU countries', though without EEA or Single Market membership. Low access means trading under WTO rules with no further agreement.

A third column gives the total amounts estimated by OW to be at risk in the event of exit with the lowest access, which includes the market infrastructure, or 'ecosystem' of related and dependent services, which they think will necessarily also be affected.[9] As can be seen, the potential losses to the ecosystem are much larger than those arising from the loss of financial services directly, though no data sources or citations are given to show from where these ecosystem estimates have been drawn – a grievous omission.

Table 16.4: Estimates of Costs of Post-Brexit outcomes: high and low access extremes

	High access	Low access	+ costs to 'ecosystem'
Revenue £bn	2	19	35
Jobs	3,500	33,000	70,000
Gross Value Added	0.5	10.5	20
Tax revenue £bn	< 0.5	4	9

Source: p.14, Oliver Wyman, Sept 2016, op.cit

Known unknowns: how will the parties involved respond?

Whether the eventual Brexit agreement provides high or low access post-Brexit depends on how parties involved respond in their new circumstances.

- **UK-based banks:** may decide that, on balance, subsidiaries are a reasonable alternative to passporting. HSBC, Barclays, RBS and Lloyds already have authorised subsidiaries elsewhere in the EEA which themselves currently passport into London. Two more types of passport, which follow G20 and Financial Stability Board (FSB) initiatives, and are open to third countries, are due to come into effect in January 2018. In addition, already enacted EU and UK legislation allows banks of third countries deemed 'equivalent' to conduct certain designated financial activities in the EU.[10] Unless, therefore, the EU decided that UK regulatory legislation though identical is not equivalent to the EU version, certain UK financial services would be unaffected by Brexit.[11] However, no-one knows how feasible or cost effective or extensive these 'alternatives' and 'equivalents' might prove to be. Each of the many banks in the City of London will have to decide according to their own circumstances.

- **ECB and EU finance ministers:** may decide to press for a prohibition on clearing euro-denominated instruments anywhere but in the eurozone, in which case it will 'serve as a lesson' not just to the British, but also to Americans, Japanese, Chinese and indeed the whole world. And what will that lesson be? That the euro is no longer intended to be a global reserve currency? That the EU intends to be a protectionist bloc in which political preferences will likely influence future regulatory decisions? The consequences of telling investors where to clear are difficult to predict, especially if they know that the regulatory authority is close kin of an assertive and ambitious tax authority.

- **EU-based financial services:** that earn substantial amounts by providing their services to the UK might be reluctant to support measures that are intended to punish the UK but which might simultaneously punish them.[12]

- **EU negotiators:** might or might not wish to forget that the EU is committed, under articles 131 to 134 of the Treaty of Rome, to the 'progressive abolition of restrictions on international trade' and, under Article 8 of the TFEU, to maintaining 'a special relationship with neighbouring countries'. They also risk turning their backs on the OECD's legally binding Code of Liberalization of Capital movements and the WTO General Agreements of Trade and Services (GATS),[13] as well as bypassing the work of the G20 and Financial Stability Board (FSB) on detailed aspects of equivalence regimes on a global level.[14]

- **EU regulators and investors:** might feel that uprooting clearing houses abruptly risks technical dislocation on a large scale, and given the vast sums involved on a daily basis, entails significant risks which not all EU financial centres might wish, or be ready, to incur. If bullish fintech promoters are to be believed, they may well in any case be relocating an obsolescent technology.[15]

The media rhetoric of the risks and possible losses that the UK financial services might suffer because of Brexit has been running far ahead of the evidence, and of the uncertainties surrounding its implementation.[16] With the OW estimates, in Table 16.4, for instance, it is not surprisingly the highest estimate of 70,000 jobs at risk which made the headlines, especially in the Remain press. One has also to recognize that it is in the interest of financial institutions presently located in London to talk up the worst possible outcomes, to make sure the UK government is listening, and to persuade them to make concessions that will leave them undisturbed, allowing others to bear the costs of Brexit. As they respond to the EU position, the UK negotiators have to answer a number of other questions.

- **UK negotiators:** have to decide how far they should go to preserve passporting or clearing in their present form. Even if Brexit were cancelled tomorrow, it is hardly likely that the UK would remain the financial centre of a monetary union to which it does not wish to belong, and is set on path of greater integration in which it would not participate. Would it retain its primacy in EU clearing indefinitely, even if there were no Brexit?[17]

- **UK Government:** as a whole has to consider how far it is reasonable to expect UK taxpayers to help banks they rescued just a few years ago. Weren't voters told at that time of the need to rebalance the UK economy and curb its excessive dependence on financial services? Might not some reduction in EU-related financial services contribute to this end?

Are other service sectors at risk?

The only other service sector to identify the benefit of the Single Market for them, and to voice their concerns about leaving it, is aviation. The European Common Aviation Area (ECAA) enables any EU airline to fly between any two points in Europe, and therefore bears a certain resemblance to the bankers' passport, though it is not directly linked to EU membership. The ECAA has 36 member countries who must be prepared to 'accept EU aviation laws' and to 'establish a framework of close economic cooperation… with the EU', neither of which would not seem to be insurmountable objections for the UK, though any one signatory state could object to the amendment to allow continued UK participation.[18]

Transport does not, moreover, earn a large trade surplus for the UK, as Table 16.5 shows. UK negotiators therefore have a rather better bargaining hand than in sectors where there is a far more pronounced UK surplus. Any attempt to restrict the access of UK airlines to the ECAA would be perceived as a blatant attempt to punish the UK at the expense of a mutually beneficial trading relationship, and probably be opposed by host countries of several EU member airlines that operate from the UK.

Table 16.5 shows UK services exports to the EU28 in 2015, along with the imports and the balance of payments for each sector. The travel sector is an example of the way in which sector figures may hide considerable sub-sector variations. Under an overall deficit of £10 billion, it includes education which earned a substantial surplus of just under £7 billion in 2015.

Table 16.5: UK exports to and imports from EU28 by sector, in order of payments surplus, 2014

Service sector	Exports £bn	As % of world exports	Imports £bn	Balance £bn
Financial Services	19.0	41	4.0	15.0
Insurance & pensions	6.6	35	0.6	6.0
Other business	19.7	32	14.6	5.2
Intellectual property	4.7	39	2.0	2.7
Telecom, Computer & Info	7.4	45	5.7	1.7
Transportation	11.0	45	10.0	1.0
Personal, cultural & recreational	0.0	2	0.5	-0.4
Construction	1.0	36	1.4	-0.4
Government	0.6	23	1.8	-1.2
Travel	12.1	43	22.1	-10.1
Total	84.4	39	63.3	21.1*

*total includes minor sectors excluded from table

Source: Table 9.10 ONS Pink Book

17

Other dashed hopes and unfounded claims: the Single Market in retrospect

1. Productivity gains that did not occur

Before joining the European Economic Community (EEC) the UK government claimed that membership of the enlarged community would 'lead to much improved efficiency and productivity in British industry'.[1] In 1988 the Cecchini report, the founding charter of the Single Market, predicted GDP gains of up to 6.5 or 7 per cent over five or six years after its creation.[2]

These claims, that EU or Single Market membership would improve UK productivity, are often forgotten. A few months before the referendum the former chancellor received extensive media coverage when drawing attention to the UK's low productivity. Though at that point he never suggested that faith placed in the Single Market on this score might have been misplaced, by the time of the referendum he decided they were intimately linked, and that if the UK voted for Brexit, UK GDP and productivity would fall sharply. Wolfgang Münchau's difficulty in finding the contribution of membership to productivity was mentioned earlier.

Two academic EU enthusiasts, authors of the popular British text *The European Union: Economics and Policies*, decided in their seventh edition that the idea the Single Market 'would transform EU economic performance has proved to be wide of the mark: there is no indication in the growth of output or productivity… that would support this contention'.[3]

An article by Eichengreen and Boltho was widely cited over the years before the referendum in the (mistaken) belief that it demonstrated the considerable economic benefits of the Single

Market. After noting that in 2002 the European Commission had admitted that Cecchini's predictions had not been realised and that the overall positive impact of the Single Market had been in the order of 1.5 to 2 per cent of GDP, Eichengreen and Boltho decided that 'as an upper estimate... perhaps half of the gains, as estimated by the commission in 2002, might not have been obtained in its absence'. In the absence, that is, of the Single Market. Their upper estimate of the gains from the Single Market by 2008 is therefore around one per cent of EU GDP. They did not try to estimate whether this gain was equally shared amongst EU members, nor say anything about its costs.[4] One EU enthusiast in the UK, who obviously did not read the article carefully, used this as the empirical foundation of his characterisation of the Single Market as the EU's Crown Jewel.[5]

It remains, nevertheless, important to try to find the contribution the Single Market might have made to UK GDP and productivity, since much of the grief of the Remainers, like the FT columnist Martin Wolf, seems to be about the losses in GDP and productivity that they think the UK will suffer over future years, especially if it were to choose, or be obliged, to trade under WTO rules.[6]

Figure 17.1 compares the mean GDP growth of the EU12 over the years of the UK's EU membership from 1973 to 2015, in constant 2010 US dollars, with the three kinds of non-member countries. All three of them, the graph shows, have grown significantly more than the mean of the EU12. Yet again, the Treasury estimate that trading under WTO rules would be the worst post-Brexit option is belied by the record of what has actually happened.

There is little evidence that EEC/EU membership has contributed much to the growth of founder members' GDP, though the two EEA members might be used to make a case for the Single Market and a soft Brexit. That case would rest effectively on Norway, since its GDP is over 20 times the size of Iceland's, but will have to wait until there is a reliable measure of the contribution of oil to the increase of its GDP.

On the face of things, Single Market membership does not seem to have helped GDP, but of course, GDP growth has been determined by many factors, and the links between those factors have still to be investigated and analysed. This is a task which the Treasury should

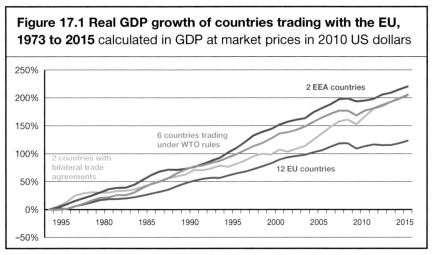

Figure 17.1 Real GDP growth of countries trading with the EU, 1973 to 2015 calculated in GDP at market prices in 2010 US dollars

Note: The six countries trading with the EU under WTO rules are Australia, Canada, Japan, Korea, (though a bilateral agreement with the EU came into force in 2011), Singapore and the United States. The 2 EEA member countries are Norway and Iceland. The two countries with bilateral agreements are Turkey and Switzerland. The 12 members of the EU are the founding members of the Single Market. Source: World Bank, World Development Indicators, GDP at market prices in constant 2010 US$.

have been engaged on over years past. Had it done so, it might have been be able to make well-founded observations during the referendum debate about the impact of the Single Market on UK GDP growth. Instead of making their wild claims about how EU and Single Market membership will continue to contribute to the growth of UK GDP to 2030, while leaving it and trading with the EU either as an EEA member, or under a bilateral treaty, or under WTO rules will lead to lower rates of GDP growth.

There aren't, as far as I recall, many amusing moments in the Treasury analysis, but in following the argument to see how it arrived at its estimates of the declining productivity post-Brexit, it is difficult not to smile. It starts from the common observation of the correlations between the level of both trade and FDI and productivity, and argues, quite acceptably, that they are causally related to some degree. It then estimates the elasticity of productivity to both trade and FDI, then estimates the impact of the shock of Brexit (half that of the great financial crisis) on trade and on FDI, then estimates from about a dozen variables, including the exchange rate, inflation, financial market volatility and employment, that 'the negative transition effects' will persist 'into the long term' with a persistent negative effect of one per cent of GDP. A tour de force of speculation, no doubt about it.

Table 17.1: Real growth of GDP of the 12 founder members of the Single Market, 1973-2014

Ireland	487%
Luxembourg	316%
Spain	146%
UK	135%
Netherlands	134%
Portugal	130%
France	123%
Belgium	121%
Germany	110%
Denmark	94%
Italy	89%
Greece	62%

Source. World Bank, *op.cit*

Table 17.2: Percentage growth of GDP per capita, 1993-2015 in 22 OECD countries based on purchasing power parity in international dollars

	% growth
Ireland	2.55
Norway	1.88
Luxembourg	1.65
Australia	1.37
Finland	1.36
Portugal	1.33
New Zealand	1.32
Netherlands	1.31
Spain	1.30
Sweden	1.27
Denmark	1.25
Germany	1.21
Austria	1.20
Switzerland	1.19
UK	1.17
EU mean	1.14
Belgium	1.11
US	1.11
Canada	1.09
France	1.07
Greece	0.87
Italy	0.79
Japan	0.73

Source: World Bank, International Comparison Program database http://siteresources.worldbank.org/ICPEXT/Resources/ICP_2011.html

From atop this tower of estimates, its peroration begins with an understatement: 'As there is no precedent for an economy like the UK leaving the EU, any quantitative analysis is subject to uncertainty.' It then picks up confidence, stating: 'This challenge is addressed by using a set of realistic assumptions, many of them cautious, alongside empirically-based estimates...' It ends with the rousing flourish: '...to provide a rigorous and objective economic analysis of the long-term impact of remaining a member of the EU compared to the alternatives.'[7] Armed with this 'rigorous and objective economic analysis' the then chancellor then predicted the dire consequences of Brexit for UK GDP and their incomes, and Martin Wolf of the *Financial Times* and other Remain commentators spread the word. It wasn't credible, and by many accounts, the British people didn't believe it.

Table 17.1 gives the real growth of individual EU12 countries and shows that the UK did relatively well, with GDP grow over these years by 135 per cent, 15 points above the EU mean of 120 per cent. This is, however, still well short of the 200 per cent growth of the six non-EU OECD countries that never enjoyed the benefits of Single Market membership.

GDP growth per capita is the more helpful statistic when considering the impact of the Single Market on people's living standards, and seemed to be in Martin's Wolf's mind when predicting that the post-Brexit UK would be 'poorer and meaner'.

Table 17.2 of per capita growth of GDP from 1993 to 2015 does not suggest that the UK has benefited greatly from Single Market membership. It ranks 15th overall with 10 EU members, and four non-members, registering higher rates of growth, though one might draw some comfort from the fact that the UK is marginally above the EU mean, and a little more decidedly ahead of both the US and Canada.

Some commentators have claimed that these figures show that EU and Single Market membership has benefited the UK, since it is after all above the EU mean, and above the U.S. over these years, and over the years since the Single Market began.[8] They apparently feel able to draw this conclusion even before knowing how much of this UK productivity growth should be attributed to the reforms of the Thatcher era, to de-regulation, large-scale privatisation, to abusing state aid for lame ducks, and the impact of a continuously high rate of FDI coming into the UK. They therefore do not mention any of these things. Believers in the Single Market are sometimes like believers in the Soviet Union before them. A tiny speck of good news is sufficient, and normal critical standards are forgotten.

If the Single Market had had some beneficial impact on the GDP of its members one might expect to see some indication of a shared benefit, of a collective dynamic shared by its members. There is none.

The Single Market is supposed to have enabled member countries to have reaped advantages of competition and of scale. One would expect to see this most clearly in the measure of growth of GDP per person employed in the economy. Table 17.3 gives the data from 1993 to 2014, comparing the EU15 with nine other countries which have varying trade relationships with the EU. All countries in each group are ranked by their productivity in 1993, and the CAGR over the 22 years alongside the actual dollar value of the output per person employed in both 1993 and 2014. The final column gives the change in the rank order prompted by their growth over the 22 years.

From a UK point of view, the results are startling. They show the very low output per person, or productivity of the UK labour force, both at the start of the Single Market and in 2014, the most recent year available. While the UK's CAGR of 1.54 per cent over the 22 years makes it third fastest among the EU15, and in joint fifth place among the 24 countries, this has not been sufficient to move it from being ranked 13th place in the EU15, just above Greece and Portugal.

The means for each group, weighted by their population over these years, indicate that the best performance, were we to accept a mean of just two cases, is that of the two countries having a bilateral agreements with the EU. However, with 15 cases, there can be no doubt that, like the earlier graph of GDP growth of the EU12, the performance of the EU15 is the worst. Still no sign of any shared growth dynamic.

The OECD provides a third measure of productivity, by showing in percentage terms how far the productivity of each member country falls short of, or exceeds, that of the US in terms of output

Table 17.3: Real growth of GDP per person employed, 1993 to 2014

Ranked by productivity in 1993 (constant 2011 PPP US dollars)

Country	US$ in 1993	CAGR %	US$ in 2014	Change in rank order '93 to '14
Under WTO rules [mean CAGR 1.4%]				
US	79002	1.56	109314	-
Canada	66799	1.01	82524	-1
Australia	65542	1.36	86972	+1
Japan	59435	0.95	72523	-
New Zealand	52992	1.01	65440	-
Bilateral agreements [mean CAGR 1.8%]				
Switzerland	79544	0.77	93491	-
Turkey	37867	1.94	56666	-
EEA members [mean CAGR 1.1 %]				
NOR	98916	1.10	124555	-
ISL	51946	1.48	70671	-
EU 15 [mean CAGR 0.9 %]				
Luxembourg	149017	1.45	201748	-
Italy	82220	0.27	87013	-6
Belgium	82051	0.88	98644	-
France	77198	0.72	89701	-
Spain	74965	0.46	82548	-6
Netherlands	72122	0.79	85121	-3
Austria	69648	1.08	87198	-1
Germany	69496	0.91	84050	-2
Ireland	67456	2.08	103880	+7
Denmark	67128	1.25	87167	+3
Finland	59538	1.54	82025	-1
Sweden	59028	1.92	87961	+7
UK	55247	1.54	76161	-
Greece	54537	1.39	72824	-
Portugal	44267	1.13	56078	-

Source: World Bank World DataBank World Development Indicators (accessed at http://databank.worldbank.org/data/reports on 13.09.2016)

per member of the labour force, or per hour worked, rather than per capita, or per person employed. Table 17.4 shows how the gap has narrowed or widened under the Single Market years from 1993 to 2013.

One member country, Luxembourg, has a positive productivity gap with the US in 1993, though in comparisons of industrial productivity it bears more resemblance to an offshore financial centre than to a normal industrial economy. Three other member countries have seen the gap narrow: Ireland most strikingly, Portugal by over five percentage points, and Denmark by nearly three points. The other eight member countries, which include the larger EU economies, have all fallen back in terms of productivity versus the US, most by rather small amounts, though Belgium by more than 13 percentage points, Italy by more than 11, and the UK, the third largest decline, by six, which rather spoils the modestly favourable impression given by the preceding measure of GDP growth per capita.

This measure does not suggest that the Single Market programme has had a distinctive and positive impact on productivity which was shared by all its members. Like the others, they suggest that a country's productivity is primarily in its own hands, though Ireland strongly suggests that foreign investors are a big help.[9]

Table 17.4: Are the members of the Single Market closing the productivity gap with the US? 1993 to 2013

Percentage gap in GDP per hour worked with respect to the USA

	1993	2013	% change
Ireland	-30.1	-6.8	+23.3
Portugal	-52.6	-47.4	+5.2
Denmark	-8.5	-5.7	+2.8
Luxembourg	41.3	41.9	+0.6
France	-6.5	-6.9	-0.4
Greece	-45.8	-46.3	-0.5
Germany	-5.7	-6.9	-1.2
Spain	-21.4	-23.4	-2.0
Netherlands	-2.1	-5.0	-2.9
UK	-19.8	-25.8	-6.0
Italy	-13.2	-24.3	-11.1
Belgium	11.7	-1.6	-13.3

Source: OECD Dataset: GDP per capita and productivity levels, Gap in GDP per hour worked with respect to the USA 1993 and 2013, www.oecd.ilibrary.org/statistics

Trying to identify the contribution the Single Market may have made to the productivity of the UK, over the life of the Single Market would be an extended and demanding research task but, as they stand, none of these measures of productivity give any reason to think that it has made a noticeable contribution. If it has made any contribution at all, it is difficult to believe it would be anything but marginal, and hardly sufficient to make one regret the UK decision to leave the Single Market.

2. Foreign investors that were not enthused

A considerable literature has developed to find and rate the determinants of foreign investment decisions, and to plot how they change over time and place. They usually include a large number of determinants which, as it happens, seldom include the Single Market.[10] UNCTAD, who have been collecting the data about them since 1970, have been consistently cautious, and refer to the determinants only in the most general terms.[11]

At the time of the debate about UK euro entry, there were frequent plausible sounding warnings about the flight of foreign investment if the UK failed to join. They proved to be spectacularly wrong. FDI in the UK subsequently increased at a faster rate than in the rest of the EU. Remain supporters nonetheless decided to resurrect the argument for the referendum debate. The argument also seemed to be a favourite of Sir John Major. He and others claimed that they knew that Single Market membership has been an important, even decisive, factor in the case of making investments into the UK, and that FDI would decline after the UK left the EU.

The Treasury incorporated an estimated decline of between 18 and 26 per cent of FDI inflows over the 15 years of its 'modelling horizon'. Since there is no knowing what action a post-Brexit government might take to encourage more FDI, and separating the appeal of the UK *per se* from its appeal as a member of Single Market is fiendishly difficult, this could be no more than a guess.[12]

For some years now, it has been clear that the EU has not been particularly attractive to foreign investors. A staff contribution to the European Commission's 'Single Market Review' in 2007 pointed out: 'Since 2001 the volume of FDI from the rest of the world into the EU25 has gradually declined… the Internal Market has not been able to deliver in terms of promoting further the role of the EU with respect to global investment flows… [and] is also losing its attractiveness for international R&D investment.'[13]

Since the financial crisis a small literature has emerged to try to understand why, as an OECD report in 2014 put it, in 'the world minus EU', global investment flows 'had fully recovered and were setting new records already in 2010', while in the EU the decline continued. The decline in its view was not confined to the weaker Mediterranean economies, but on the contrary 'concentrated in the largest: France, Germany, and the UK'. The report concluded that 'one thing is clear: the collapse in international investment flows in Europe, both outward and inward, is more than just a passing cyclical phenomenon… and it's time to sound the alarm'.[14] Sir John Major and other Remain supporters evidently didn't hear it.

In Figure 17.2 the 2014 per capita value of inward stock for 14 countries is shown in the columns. The colour indicates their trading relationship with the EU. The red columns are countries which trade with the EU under WTO terms, the green columns are countries with bilateral agreements with the EU, the orange are the two countries within the EEA, while the blue are members of the EU.[15] The dots show the change as a percentage from 2004 to 2014.

While two EU member countries, Ireland and the UK, as well as two EEA countries with membership access to the Single Market, have comparatively high levels of FDI stock, independent countries with small markets are not at a noticeable disadvantage. Three of them Israel, Switzerland and Singapore had, along with Iceland, the fastest growing receipts of FDI from 2004 to 2014. If the Single Market itself had been a major attraction for foreign investors, one would expect both the mean EU15 per capita stock, and its growth over the eleven years, to have been higher than they are.[16] EU membership is certainly not a decisive determinant, though it might be a contributory factor, *ceteris paribus*. In any event, it would be unwise to make confident claims. In 1980, the earliest year for which the UNCTAD publishes data of the inward stock of countries, the value of the UK FDI stock was 28 per cent of the total value for original EEC six. In 2015 it was 31 per cent. So we can say that 23 years of Single Market membership have not made a lot of difference.

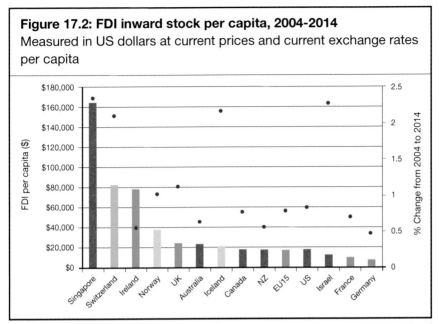

Figure 17.2: FDI inward stock per capita, 2004-2014

Measured in US dollars at current prices and current exchange rates per capita

Source: UNCTAD; Foreign direct investment: Inward and outward flows and stock, annual, 1980-2014.
Graphic by Christian Stensrud

3. World-wide trade agreements of marginal significance

One of the more misleading claims made by Remain campaigners was that, by virtue of its 'clout' and 'heft', the EU had negotiated 36 trade agreements with third countries around the world which would take post-Brexit UK years and even decades to re-negotiate and amend, if indeed it could do so at all. Leaving the EU would, it was claimed, disrupt UK trade, and risk significant temporary, or even permanent, losses for UK exporters.

Clearly none of those who made this argument had ever examined the WTO listing of the trade agreements that the EU has concluded over the past 43 years. They have three striking characteristics.

- First, the EU has consistently **preferred to negotiate with small states**. Korea, Mexico and Turkey are the three largest partner countries, but the mean size of the GDP of all EU partner countries in 2014 was $191 billion which is a little less than the GDP of Peru. By contrast, the mean size of the trade partners of Chile in 2014 was $2,965 billion, of Korea's partners was $4,396 billion, of Switzerland's $23,223 billion and of Singapore's $39,572 billion.

- Second, they **rarely include Commonwealth countries** which might perhaps have offered good prospects for UK exports. The GDP of all the Commonwealth countries is $7491.27 billion, but the EU has trade agreements with Commonwealth countries whose aggregate GDP in 2014 was $473.92 billion, which is about six per cent of the Commonwealth's total GDP.

- Their third characteristic is that **only two thirds of them include services**, while 90 per cent or more of the agreements of Chile, Korea, Singapore and Switzerland include services. The total market size of all the services trade agreements concluded by the EU and in force in 2016, in 2014 GDP, was $4.1tn. Those of Switzerland totalled $35.8tn. Those of Singapore totalled $37.2tn. Those of Korea totalled $40tn. Chile's at $55.4tn have a total over ten times larger than that of the EU.

Largely as a result of the three characteristics mentioned, the 34 EU trade agreements currently in force with 58 countries, offer very limited coverage to help UK exporters. Leaving aside the EFTA countries, the EU's current partner countries took 6.1 per cent of all UK goods exports in 2014 and 1.8 per cent of all UK services exports, so they could hardly have had a major impact on UK exports.[17]

Since neither the UK government nor the European Commission has tried to measure their impact on individual member countries, no one knows how effective they may have been for the UK.[18] A pilot evaluation, on the impact of EU trade agreements for UK exports, compared the growth in the value of UK exports before and after each agreement came into force. There were 15 EU agreements for which at least five years of data before and after was available, and they were compared with as many agreements as were available meeting the same conditions, from four non-EU countries. The results are given in the Table 17.5.

Ten of the 15 EU agreements saw UK exports fall post-agreement. This compares unfavourably with the scores of Korea, Singapore and Switzerland as shown, though not with Chile. Chile was,

Table 17.5: A Scorecard for FTA effectiveness
Export growth before & after agreements came into force in
5 countries

Country	No of agreements examined	Pre-agreement mean growth (CAGR) %	Post-agreement mean growth (CAGR) %	No of post-agreement gains	No of post-agreement falls	Gain/fall ratio
Chile	17	16.0	7.4	5	12	-0.4
Korea	5	3.3	6.8	4	1	4
Singapore	12	8.3	13	8	4	2
Switzerland	15	2.6	7.2	11	4	2.75
UK (EU)	15	5.0	3.6	5	10	-0.5

Source: United Nations Commodity Trade Statistics Database, COMTRADE. www.comtrade.un.org

however, somewhat exceptional. The mean rates of growth for its exports to many of its partners before it signed agreements was far higher than the other countries, and in several cases above 30 per cent per annum, so that even though it experienced the most post-agreement falls, its mean post-agreement growth is exceeded only by Singapore. It is double that of the UK.

The strategy behind EU trade agreements over the past 43 years has, from a British point of view, been misdirected. They have secured limited coverage and, as far as we can tell, have had little or no impact on export growth. Nonetheless, they have somehow or other been portrayed by many British commentators as a great benefit of EU membership.[19] Many of the 38 British companies and trade associations that contributed to the Balance of Competences Review of 2013 warmly supported them, though one suspects many of them did so because they thought T-TIP was around the corner. Clearly, none of them could have looked at the European Commission's record over the previous 40 plus years as a whole, or tried to measure the effectiveness of EU agreements for UK exports as a whole or even for themselves.

Their ill-considered commendations seem to have encouraged Remain campaigners to warn of the immense burden of re-negotiating the 36 EU trade agreements with 58 countries, which it was said, would stretch UK resources to breaking point, extend over many years, and which might in any case result in the UK being rebuffed by many partner countries.

On close inspection, this renegotiation task seems rather more manageable. Adding the 8.1 per cent of UK goods exports, and the 7.2 per cent of UK services exports going to the EFTA countries, the UK will have to renegotiate with countries receiving 14.2 per cent of its goods exports, and just under nine per cent of its services.

However, just over 80 per cent of the 14.2 per cent of goods exports covered by EU agreements are with the six countries shown in Table 17.6. If the UK's post-Brexit negotiators successfully renegotiated the first two, they would secure more than 60 per cent of the market value of all the agreements concluded by the EU in 43 years, a staggering fact. It is the same with services. Services exports to Switzerland and Norway alone account for more than 80 per cent of the value of all the services markets covered by all EU agreements in 43 years.

Table 17.6: The post-Brexit burden of trade agreement re-negotiation

Partner country	% of total UK exports to all EU partner countries	Value in 2015 US$bn	Real growth (CAGR) 1993-2015
Switzerland	49.45%	32.23	10.74%
Korea	10.96%	7.14	8.47%
Turkey	8.19%	5.34	5.72%
Norway	7.31%	4.77	3.46%
Egypt	2.30%	1.50	5.06%
Israel	2.23%	1.45	0.45%

Sources: WTO http://rtais.wto.org/; IMF Direction of Trade stats http://data.imf.org/

Moreover, renegotiations are unlikely to be especially onerous. Tariffs on non-agricultural goods of many of these partner countries for third countries are trivial, and it is not even certain that they would require any renegotiation. Some agreements are so-called 'mixed competence' agreements, meaning member countries as well as the EU, are parties to them. The Korean agreement, for instance, 'would not require any renegotiation of the substantive provisions of the FTA: all that would be needed would be a statement by the UK that it intended after Brexit to continue to operate the terms of the FTA between itself and Korea, and an acknowledgement by Korea that it would likewise continue to do so.'[20]

4. The catastrophe of high and severe unemployment

Since the financial crisis of 2008, media reports in the UK have drawn attention to the previously unthinkable rates of unemployment found in a number of the Mediterranean EU countries. This may have conveyed the impression that these rates are recent occurrences when in fact they have been an enduring characteristic of the Single Market since its beginning, and not only in the Mediterranean countries.

Figure 17.3 compares the mean rate of unemployment of its 12 founder members over the life of the Single Market with eight other OECD countries which are not EU members and whose unemployment record since 1993 is published in harmonised annual rates. In 2015, they had a combined population of 671.4 million versus the EU12's population of 380.9 million.

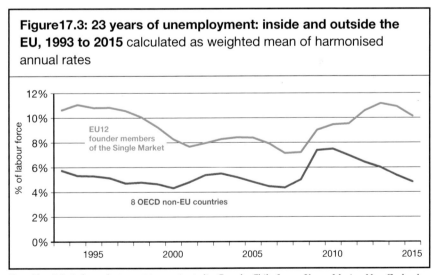

Figure17.3: 23 years of unemployment: inside and outside the EU, 1993 to 2015 calculated as weighted mean of harmonised annual rates

Note: The eight independent countries are Australia, Canada, Chile, Japan, Korea, Mexico, New Zealand and the United States. Source: OECD Employment database http://www.oecd.org

Over the first 23 years of the Single Market, its 12 founding members have had rates of unemployment getting on for double that of the OECD 8. Their mean rate was 9.4 per cent while that of OECD countries was 5.4 per cent, a startling contrast that has never been investigated and explained. It is worth underlining that these differences are not the result of the financial crisis, and that they refer to the founder members of the Single Market, not to the late entrants. Had the latter EU entrants been included, the differences would have been far greater.

Figure 17.4 compares the rates of long-term unemployment in the 12 EU countries with the other eight OECD countries for which there is age-specific data from 1993 to 2015. Long-term unemployment is here defined as being unemployed for a year or more, and is expressed in the graph, first in the darker lines, as percentages of the total unemployed in the two groups of countries, and second in the lighter lines, as percentages of all the unemployed 15 to 24-year-olds.

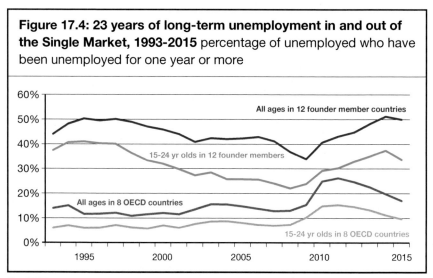

Figure 17.4: 23 years of long-term unemployment in and out of the Single Market, 1993-2015 percentage of unemployed who have been unemployed for one year or more

The OECD countries: Australia, Canada, Israel, Japan, Korea, Mexico, New Zealand and the United States.
Source: OECD iLibrary Employment and Labour Market Statistics Unemployment by duration Labour force statistics by sex and age: indicators DOI: 10.1787/lfs-data-en

Throughout these years the proportion of the unemployed of all ages suffering this fate in the EU12 has been a substantially larger proportion in the EU, often more than double that of the eight

OECD countries. The average of the EU over the 23 years is 44.7 per cent, while that of the independent countries is 15.6 per cent, and among 15 to 24-year-olds the EU average is 31.8 per cent, *more than three times* the 8.7 per cent average of the other OECD countries. Coming of age and entering the labour market has been a stressful and depressing experience for more young people in the EU than elsewhere.

That such large differences have continued over 23 years gives the impression that we are dealing with two sets of economies that differ from one another in some fundamental and enduring manner. Leaders of some EU countries are fond of claiming that they do differ from other capitalist countries by virtue of their 'social model'. One of the first questions raised by these graphs is whether this 'social model' is in some way related to these unemployment rates. They raise other questions, how has the European Commission and the Directorate-General for Employment escaped accountability given the billions of euros allocated to its employment programmes?[21] Why hasn't unemployment been the overriding pan-EU theme in elections to the European Parliament over these years?

The EU response contrasts strikingly with the urgency and energy with which the new President of the United States has addressed the problem, by repeatedly drawing it to media attention, by threatening and pressuring those he deems responsible and, on his third day in office, by withdrawing from Trans Pacific Partnership because he thinks it might make it worse. The current rate of unemployment in the United States is 4.9 per cent. The current EU unemployment rate is 8.5 per cent.

In the Brexit context, these contrasts raise other questions. Why is it that so many UK politicians, including Scotland's First Minister, many commentators as well as voters, including Leave voters, want the UK to remain in the Single Market post-Brexit?[22] It has managed, over some 23 years, to normalise the misery of unemployment on an unprecedented scale, especially for its young people. What, one wonders, could be the secret of its appeal?

18

A summary of the evidence

Starting points of the investigation

This analysis has sought to discover the benefits of membership of the Single Market for UK exports of goods and services over the past 23 years, and to compare these benefits with the export performance of countries that have other kinds of trading relationship with the EU. Successive UK governments never sought to monitor and analyse those benefits, so there are no authoritative official UK or EU sources to which we can refer. The Treasury's hurried attempt to identify them during the referendum campaign by means of models was, for many reasons, found to be untrustworthy.

This analysis therefore examined evidence from seven major international agencies (the OECD, the IMF, UN Comtrade, the ITC, UNCTAD, the WTO and the World Bank) that have been routinely collecting data about world trade and the economic performance of the UK, the EU and other countries over these years.

Their data about the growth of UK exports since the Single Market was formally inaugurated on 1st January 1993 is especially important, because export growth has been the main expected benefit of the Single Market for the UK. It was the main reason for originally joining the Common Market, for the formation of the Single Market, and for UK participation in it. It must also be one of the main concerns of UK Brexit negotiators, and will no doubt be one of the main criteria by which observers will decide whether the decision to withdraw from the Single Market was sensible or, for that matter, whether it is wise for the Scottish Government to try remain a member.

These databases allow comparisons over time to be made with

other nations that have not enjoyed the benefits and advantages of Single Market membership, and these comparisons are one of the best ways by which benefits of membership of the Single Market for the UK can be identified and measured. Likewise, comparisons with countries which have been exporting to the EU under WTO rules allow us to decide whether, if the UK fails to secure a good deal with the EU, trading with the EU under WTO rules is an acceptable option.

Summaries of the main findings

- An extrapolation of growth of UK goods exports to the other EU members over the Common Market decades from 1973 to 1992 placed alongside real growth over the Single Market years from 1993 to 2015 shows that the rapid growth of the Common Market was not continued. The Single Market has been an era of slow and declining growth of UK goods exports to other members.

- When ranked among the top 40 fastest-growing larger exporters of goods to the EU from 1993 to 2015, the UK finishes 36th. The fact that many non-member countries' exports have grown at a faster rate throws doubt on the notion that the UK has benefited greatly from membership, and that non-members have been at a disadvantage.

- While UK intra-EU exports have grown more slowly than those of most other members, the growth rate of EU12 exports to each other is also slow when compared with that of other G20 countries, of other OECD countries, and of the largest exporters from around the world. These comparisons throw more doubt on the supposed benefits of membership, and on the disadvantages of non-membership.

- Countries exporting to the EU under WTO rules dominate the rankings of the fastest growing exporters to it, and their real growth rates exceed that of countries which trade with the EU under bilateral treaties, or as EEA members, or as fellow EU members. This evidence therefore directly contradicts the Treasury estimates of the relative benefits of these three trade relationships for post-Brexit UK. Those exporting under WTO rules have been the most successful exporters to the EU under the Single Market, not the least.

- A synoptic view of the goods exports of nations trading with the EU under four different relationships – as members, as EEA members, with bilateral agreements and as countries trading only under WTO rules – shows that UK exports had more rapid growth than all the others during the Common Market years from 1973 to 1992. However, it has slower growth than all the others during the Single Market years from 1993 to 2015. This reinforces doubts about the supposed benefits of the Single Market.

- Over the entire 43 years of membership the UK's real compound annual growth rate of 2.65 per cent is virtually the same as the 12 founder members of the Single Market as a whole (2.64 per cent) and of 13 countries trading under WTO rules (2.63 per cent). Thus, the benefits of EU membership for the UK exports over 43 years by comparison with 13 countries trading under WTO rules has been 0.02 per cent CAGR and 2 per cent in total real growth over the 43 years.

- Over the 23 years of the Single Market, UK annual export growth to Single Market countries has been very low indeed (1.0 per cent), and comfortably exceeded by those trading in every other kind of relationship, under WTO rules (1.93 per cent), as EU members (2.28 per cent) under bilateral agreements (3.58 per cent) and as EEA members (3.91 per cent). The ordinal positions do not change when measured only to the eve of the financial crisis in 2008.

- Although those trading as EEA members and with bilateral agreements invariably have the highest export growth over the Single Market years, generalizing from their experience is very high risk. Our EEA sample is de facto one country, Norway. And generalising from the experience of the two countries trading under sharply differing bilateral agreements is scarcely less so.

- Since trading under WTO rules incurs no costs it emerges as an acceptable and even attractive post-Brexit option, with real growth in exports to the EU11 only 2 per cent less than UK export growth over 43 years. During the Single Market from 1993 to 2015 real export growth to the EU11 under WTO rules was 27 per cent higher UK's.

- The UK has exported to 111 countries under WTO rules from 1993 to 2015, at a CAGR of 2.88 per cent. Its exports to the 62 countries with which the EU has trade agreements grew at a CAGR of 1.82 per cent. The slowest growth of all, at a CAGR of 0.91 per cent, has been to the 14 founder and long-standing members of the Single Market, albeit with a spike in 2006 preceding the financial crisis. Over the 23 years, UK exports to 111 countries under WTO rules have grown four times as much as its exports to the EU15 fellow members of the Single Market, 88 per cent versus 22 per cent.

- A mini case study shows the CAGR of the exports of Scotch whisky to the EU from 1993 to 2014 was 1.62 per cent, while that of Bourbon, which exported to the EU under WTO rules, was 8.6 per cent. There was a similar differential, 3.58 versus 7.68 per cent, in their exports to other countries round the world, in which Scotch is supposed to have benefited from EU trade agreements.

- Since the Scotch Whisky Association has been a hugely enthusiastic supporter of EU and its trade agreements, this suggests that trade associations may not always be the best judges of the benefits of the Single Market for the UK economy, or of the disadvantages of non-membership.

- Brexiteers' technical and procedural arguments against leaving the Single Market and trading with the EU under WTO rules ignores the success of both countries that have long been exporting to the EU under WTO rules, as well as the UK's own success in trading with the rest of the world under these rules. They have little merit.

- By the European Commission's preferred index of market integration, the difference between intra and extra EU exports as a proportion of GDP, a single market in services barely exists. Its 'high point' appears to have been reached in 2007. It has not advanced at all since then.

- Member countries' 'reserved rights' in the opening Trade in Services Agreement (TiSA) negotiations in 2013 indicate that partner countries in EU trade agreements cannot expect to enjoy access to a single market in services, even though it may be advertised as such.

- When the UK is ranked among the top 40 fastest-growing exporters of services to the EU from 2010 to 2014, it comes 25th, one place below the EU28 exporting to each other. The services exports of many non-members to the EU have therefore grown at faster rate.

- The CAGR of the services exports of 27 member countries to each other over the eight years to 2012 was 3.2 per cent, while that of 27 non-members to the EU was 3.7 per cent. If non-members exports to the Single Market have grown at a faster rate, it reinforces doubts about the existence of the single market in services, and strongly supports the UK decision to withdraw from it because it suggests that it will make little difference.

- Swiss services exports to the EU have not been handicapped by non-membership of the Single Market. On the contrary, they have grown 20 per cent more than those of the UK since 1999, and are currently more than five times larger in value per capita. However, no data is available about Swiss exports of financial services to the EU.

- Although the benefits of the Single Market cannot be observed in aggregate cross-national measures, UK-based banks have at least one identifiable and tangible benefit of Single Market membership: passporting. Clearing in euro-denominated instruments is not, in the same sense, a benefit of the Single Market, since it is currently part of a global clearing market, and it seems likely that the EU may in the future exclude the UK by limiting this clearing to eurozone members. Both these two facilities for services exporters are at risk post-Brexit.

- The best estimate to date is that 23 per cent of the financial services of the City of London are EU-related, and that 45 per cent of this is at risk post-Brexit, which in 2014 was about £13 billion in revenue, though with unknown knock-on impact on related services and, therefore, on employment and tax revenues.

- Single Market membership appears to have had no other benefits that might compensate for its failure to help the growth of UK goods and services exports. The real growth of EU12 GDP since 1973 is significantly below that of countries trading with the EU under WTO rules, under bilateral agreements, or as EEA members.

- Three measures of productivity growth, as measured by GDP per cap, GDP per person employed and GDP per cap versus US, do not give any indication that EU or Single Market membership has helped solve the UK's chronic productivity problem, or done much to help other members. While UK productivity has grown slightly faster than most EU countries, it ranked 13th among the EU15 in 1993 and 13th in 2015.

- The notion that EU or Single Market membership has boosted FDI in the UK inevitably rests on intuition and hearsay rather than evidence. After Ireland, the UK has the highest per capita FDI stock in the EU, though that is below that of a number of smaller non-member countries. The mean value of the per capita FDI stock of the EU15 is lower still, which suggests it has not been a magnet for FDI.

- Trade agreements negotiated by the European Commission over the past 43 years have been near worthless from a British point of view, being mainly with small or micro partner countries, outside the Commonwealth, with relatively few of them including services. Their coverage of UK world export markets in 2014, excluding EFTA countries, was a miniscule 6.1 per cent of UK world markets in goods and 1.8 per cent in services.

- Unemployment in the 12 founder members of the Single Market has been nearly double that of other non-EU OECD countries since 1993, while long-term unemployment, as a percentage of unemployment, for 15 to 24 year olds has been more than three times higher. From the beginning, the Single Market has demonstrated that it most definitely is not 'good for jobs', though fortunately, the UK has suffered less than most.

Limitations of the data

Before drawing conclusions from this evidence, some of its limitations should be noted. The uneven and time-limited nature of the services data has been mentioned in the text. It is also clear that, since the evidence drawn from the seven databases have not been part of any ongoing monitoring or analysis of the Single Market in the UK, this report has been unable to benefit from research that might help further explain the findings reported. As it stands, we are left in mid-air with a number of baffling and counter-intuitive findings.

- Why has the growth of UK goods exports to the Single Market been so inferior to their growth to the Common Market?

- Why have the exports of goods and services to the Single Market of countries trading under WTO rules grown faster than those of members to each other?

- Why have countries trading with the EEC/EU under WTO rules been only marginally less successful than members trading with each other over the 43 years of the UK's EU membership?

- Why have UK exports to countries under WTO rules grown faster than its exports to the EU and to countries with which the EU has trade agreements?

- Why has the single market in services failed to develop since 2007?

- Why have EU trade agreements proved to be so ineffective for the UK?

- What do the Scottish Government and many others find the Single Market appealing, when it has been accompanied by very slow UK export growth, has always had catastrophic unemployment rates, and has had no discernible impact on UK productivity?

The most important limitation of this report, however, is that almost all these findings refer to the UK as a national unit, and compare the growth of its goods and services exports over time with those of other nations. It only considered sectors within UK goods and services in two brief asides, one about Scotch whisky and the other about financial services.

The former was prompted by the common inclination of trade associations, demonstrated copiously in the Balance of Competences Review, to lend their support to both the Single Market and to the trade agreements of the EU without collecting or referring to any published evidence.

The second was prompted by the fact that even though the cross-national data for services exports did not indicate UK exports as a whole had enjoyed any particular benefit from Single Market membership, spokespersons of the UK financial services sector could provide, in passporting, a tangible, irrefutable example of a benefit of the Single Market for the banking subsector.

These two asides suggested that a fully comprehensive analysis of the benefits of the Single Market would require detailed breakdown by sectors and sub-sectors of UK exports of goods and services, supported by sectoral cross-national comparisons over time. Only then will we know whether the Single Market has brought benefits for other sectors and sub-sectors, which, like bankers' passporting, are not evident from national export data. Ideally, one would like to compare the growth of every important UK export sector with the growth of exports in those same sectors from countries trading with the EU that have had to rely on WTO rules.

Investigations of this kind should, however, have been conducted years ago, and we now must all pay the price for the reluctance of the UK government and trade associations to conduct them. However, we are where we are, and these limitations in the data should not, in themselves, allow the case for membership of the Single Market, or regret for the decision to leave, to continue, as it has for so long, resting on the impressions, opinions and say-so of influential, 'right-thinking' people with ready access to the media. Cross-national comparisons are the essential first step, and until the cross-national sectoral studies identify and document benefits that may be hidden beneath them, they provide the only clear way of comparing the relative economic benefits of trading as a member of the Single Market with those of trading bilateral treaties or under WTO rules.

19

Conclusions

The evidence presented above has, by multiple measures, failed to identify the benefits of membership of the Single Market for the growth of UK exports of goods and services, or the disadvantages for non-members who export to it. It therefore answers the question raised at the start and leads to the view that, given the costs of membership and the lack of any evidence to support its value, Theresa May's decision to withdraw from the Single Market was entirely justified on economic grounds.

The reasons are clear: while the benefits of the Single Market cannot be identified, the economic and political costs are known and burdensome: the budget contributions, the surrender of the right to negotiate trade agreements, the regulation of the entire UK economy in the interest of the small sections of it that export to the EU, and the inability to form an independent migration policy. These are in addition, of course, to the political costs of the subjection of the UK Parliament to an unaccountable law-making executive bureaucracy and to the European Court of Justice.

The EU is a unique political experiment, diametrically opposed to the fundamental principle of political authority which has come, over the 20th and 21st centuries, to be accepted across the world: that those who make and enforce the laws should be co-cultural with those who are expected to obey them. The EU is the only polity on the planet which contests this principle and, if it delivered remarkable economic benefits that were unobtainable under any other, it might perhaps succeed in doing so permanently.

However, the evidence presented above shows that the EU has not done so. It has delivered economic benefits for nineteen of its member countries, since they are recipient countries and receive transfer payments from the other nine contributing members.[1] But these might as well be delivered to them by a dedicated foreign aid programme, like the Norway Fund. Other economic benefits that it has delivered, such as the ease and convenience of trade between members, have had, at best, a modest or marginal impact on the aggregate growth of exports and, since the start of the Single Market, no impact at all on the UK exports. There is, moreover, no evidence of any collateral benefits on GDP, on productivity, on employment, or from trade agreements with third countries, and the impact on FDI remains uncertain.

One might pause, and spend time evaluating the arguments of the heterogeneous cross-section of political opinion which is committed to maintain membership of the Single Market to see if they have ever produced any evidence to demonstrate its benefits, or even, for that matter, to demonstrate that the single market in services actually exists. As it is, they are urging the British people to pay the considerable, and real, economic and political costs of remaining in the Single Market even though it has brought them no demonstrable benefits. These costs deserve further attention. The decision of the UK government to withdraw from the Single Market, and to be prepared to rely on WTO rules, is in the best interests of the British people.

20

Notes on the negotiations

Apart from helping to decide between the arguments on how the UK should trade with the EU post-Brexit, the comparative data about the export performance of the UK and others also prompts some observations on the way in which the trade aspects of the withdrawal negotiations might be conducted.

The two opening moves of the negotiations have already been made

The Government's decision that the UK will withdraw from the Single Market has in effect already opened the negotiations. In so doing, it has saved immense amounts of time and prevented negotiations becoming bogged down in complex exchanges and calculations required to identify the trade-offs and concessions that may have been offered to maintain some form of membership.

Since Mrs May has also made abundantly clear the UK commitment to free trade, we now know that it is ready to conclude a new bilateral trade agreement in order to continue its present free trade with EU members. If, however, the EU wishes to impose tariffs or other barriers on UK goods and services exports to the EU, the UK will regretfully be obliged to reciprocate by imposing similar tariffs or other barriers of equal value to similar EU exports. Reciprocity is a well-established principle in trade negotiations, so everyone will immediately know where they stand.

Judging by the comments of a number of its leaders, the EU will reply that it cannot allow an ex-member to export to its members on the same terms as current members. It will therefore have the unenviable task of preparing a list of the tariffs or non-tariff barriers that it wishes to impose on UK exports, in the full knowledge that tariffs or restrictions of similar value will be imposed on similar goods and services from its own member countries.

They will, no doubt, have a short list of the sectors which, if the UK were to reciprocate with EU tariffs, would be devastated, and will give these high priority and welcome free trade or something very close to it. So the EU might well begin with some cherry picking. In the majority of sectors, one suspects their proposed tariffs will be modest and exemplary and resemble those still imposed under the EU's present trade agreements. The scope and substance of the trade agreement will therefore largely be determined by the EU negotiators, since the UK will continuously be proposing zero tariffs and barriers. The only choice for the UK will be to decide, when the EU proposes barriers to UK exports, what EU exports should face barriers. Presumably those deemed roughly comparable and most likely to secure concessions elsewhere. This is the UK's turn to cherry pick.

These UK choices will probably provoke subsidiary negotiations between the EU negotiators and the representatives of member countries whose products or services may suddenly face tariff barriers when exporting to the UK. These member countries will, of course, know that the UK does not wish to impose any tariffs, and has only done so because the European Commission deems them necessary in the interests of the European Project as a whole. Some of the toughest, and lengthiest, negotiations might well be between member countries and the EU, rather than the UK and the EU.

In all these trade-offs, the UK negotiators have much to gain from transparency, publicity and leaks, so that their commitment to free trade becomes widely known to the people and exporters of the EU. They will then also know that if their exports face tariffs or other restrictions when exporting to the UK in the future, because either their own government or some other EU party has decided that these tariffs are in the EU's best interests. There might then be some opportunity for public opinion in the EU to influence the negotiations.

Transparency might even help to change the minds of some of those in the UK who have convinced themselves that continued membership of the Single Market is 'fundamental to our economic future'. Trade without tariff and non-tariff barriers seems to be what they value most about it.[1] The UK negotiators will be seen to be on the right side throughout, and one might add, always seeking the same trade relationship as many British people thought they were voting for in 1975.

The third move is coming shortly: the Great Repeal Bill

On 2nd October 2016 the Prime Minister promised: 'We will introduce, in the next Queen's Speech, a Great Repeal Bill that will remove the European Communities Act from the statute book.' The Secretary of State for Exiting the EU later explained that this meant that 'EU law will be transposed into domestic law, wherever practical, on exit day.'[2] From that specified day, the sole legitimate source of authority for every single rule, regulation, standard, and procedure that previously depended on an EU treaty, regulation or directive will be UK law, enforced by UK courts.

At first glance, it seems paradoxical that to obtain a clean break from the Single Market, every regulatory and institutional aspect of it that has been adopted over 23 years membership must remain in force and be incorporated into UK law. There can, however, be no doubt of the benefits of this continuity for ensuring a smooth domestic transition, for the negotiating of trade agreements with third countries, and above all, for the negotiation of an exit trade agreement with the EU.

The domestic Brexit transition will be easier because goods exporters will have the certainty of knowing that current EU technical, sanitary and phytosanitary standards for traded goods, together with the standard-setting, testing, certification and accreditation bodies that support EU conformity assessment procedures will continue to be used until such time they are expressly amended or repealed by the UK Parliament. The current EU Rules of Origin system, much as set out in the Comprehensive Economic and Trade Agreement (CETA) with Canada, will also continue to apply when required.[3]

The current tariffs will also continue, though they will probably be the first to be amended post-Brexit, when the UK starts to 'novate' or renegotiate existing EU agreements, and to negotiate new trade agreements with third countries. The EU external tariff makes it easier to blueprint proposed agreements with third countries that will be concluded after the UK withdraws. They provide a familiar baseline against which partner countries can easily identify the points which they would like an agreement with the UK to amend.

The most important benefit of this Bill is that it will drastically narrow the scope of a trade agreement with the EU required on exit day. Once passed, it will have removed much the greater part of the issues that take the time of negotiators of normal trade agreements, and therefore make it more likely that Brexit can be concluded, on schedule, with an appropriate agreement.

A fourth move, implied but not yet announced

A fourth move is implied in Mrs May's words 'that no deal for Britain is better than a bad deal', which can only mean that the UK is ready to walk away without a deal and thereafter trade with the EU under WTO rules. The evidence presented above shows that it is an acceptable option and not one that has to be feared. No doubt it is less convenient, but the UK already trades with 111 countries under these rules, and as shown above, its exports to them grew at a compound annual growth rate of 2.88 per cent from 1993 to 2015, while those to the EU14 grew at a rate of 0.91 per cent.

Other countries that trade with the EU under these rules have frequently outperformed those of the UK and of other members. Over 43 years the exports of the 14 of them, for which we have adequate data, had a compound annual growth rate of 0.02 percentage points less than the UK. Over the 23 years of the Single Market, these countries exports have grown at a compound annual growth rate but 0.93 percentage points higher than UK exports.[4] One of the great illusions surrounding the Single Market is that trading under WTO rules has been a grave disadvantage because they have not been 'sitting at the table and helping to make the rules'. The other is that there is a single market in services. The services exports to the EU, of countries trading under WTO rules, grew from 2004 to 2012 at a CAGR of 3.7 per cent, while the exports of the EU to each other grew at 3.2 per cent.

These figures should be pinned on the wall of the UK negotiators' office. They make a strong case for stating the 'no deal' option at the start of the negotiations in the form of an exit day deadline after which, whatever may have been agreed will be incorporated in a partial agreement, but the UK will apply WTO rules in the rest of its trade with the EU.

Delays: the case for a deadline and a stated default option

There have been frequent warnings that it will take many years to negotiate and conclude a trade agreement with the EU, and might even therefore make it impossible for the UK to leave the EU within two years. Some of these warnings refer to the time it has taken for the EU to negotiate trade agreements with Switzerland, Canada and other countries. Many observers have therefore argued that since the UK is a larger economy, has been involved in the EU for so many years, the negotiations will necessarily be more complex, more animated and contentious, and more prolonged.

There may be some negotiations with the EU that the UK will wish to continue for years. A few are mentioned below. However, arguments that it will be impossible to conclude a trade agreement in a couple of years, based on analogies with other EU agreements, are bound to be mistaken. The EU-UK trade agreement has no close analogies. It will be between parties with identical tariffs and non-tariff barriers, identical product regulations, and identical customs rules, which is a wholly unprecedented situation in the history of trade negotiations. There is nothing like it in the WTO Regional Trade Agreement Information System. The UK has, in effect, been negotiating this particular agreement over its entire of membership of the Single Market.

Moreover, the two parties to this agreement do not have protected interests that might be threatened by an agreement opening trade to a new source of competition. One party is withdrawing from an existing agreement but offering to continue free trade as before.

The other has to decide whether to accept the offer that free trade should continue, or whether to make a political gesture on behalf of the European project. It is not clear why this should take them months or years. It might be tricky, and require delicate handling, but it is hardly a towering intellectual challenge.

Most of the warnings, however, are not of this kind. They are expressions of hope that the negotiations will take years and years, or even decades, and seem to be intended to discourage both the Government and Brexiteers, in the hope that they might lose heart and Brexit might be reversed. They are the continuation of the campaign. EU leaders who were offended and insulted by the UK electorate's blow to their cherished project have joined in, also in the hope that the prospect of an arduous and protracted process, and the adverse effects that prolonged uncertainty might have on the UK economy, might lead to a change of mind in the UK.

One cannot therefore rule out the possibility that there will be deliberate delays, intended to punish the UK for wishing to leave the EU and to provide a 'lesson', as President Hollande put it, for other member countries that might be tempted to join the UK in its departure.[5] Tariffs and non-tariff barriers cannot be altogether effective in that respect, since they can be reciprocated, but delay, and certainly a 10-year delay, might weary the most enthusiastic Brexiteer, discourage investment and perhaps reduce UK growth and raise unemployment towards mean EU levels, helping to inflict on the British people some of the miseries predicted by the Treasury and other Remainers.[6] A sure sign that the European Commission intends to prolong the negotiations as a tactic and/ or a punishment will be when it insists on consecutive rather than concurrent negotiations on disparate issues like fishing and UK territorial waters, the UK's remaining liabilities, and the ancillary agencies discussed below.

Remainers in the UK will be working to the same end, hoping by some means to prolong the negotiations – they have already tried to delay the triggering of Article 50 – and hoping that a breakdown or suspension in the negotiations provoked by some fortuitous external event and accompanied by some severe downturn in the economy might yet provide an opportunity for another referendum.

If the negotiations could be prolonged, and the agreed terms did not finally come into force until after May 2020, when the next UK election is due, then there might indeed be a second referendum of a sort. It is the Remainers last hope, their last chance, and a very long shot.

The British negotiators will be tempted to think that mutually assured job destruction, and the adverse economic impact of extended uncertainty, will keep both sides on track and up to speed. The EU has, however, long accepted a certain amount of economic misery for its citizens in the interests of the European Project, seen in its willingness to tolerate levels of unemployment far higher than those of other OECD countries. The two parties in this negotiation are therefore by no means equal in this respect. The British side is more likely to fear increased unemployment, and is more vulnerable to the adverse effects of uncertainty.

There is, therefore, a strong case for a deadline, stated at the start of the negotiations, with a clear declaration, both to the EU and its own exporters, that the UK prefers free trade, but is ready to trade with the EU under WTO rules.

Separate, concurrent, mood-setting negotiations: UK participation in EU agencies and programmes

There are a large number of EU and European agencies and programmes in many of which non-member countries currently participate and in which the UK will most probably wish to continue participating as a contributing member. Among them are the European Medicines Agency, Maritime, Food and Airline Safety agencies, the Intellectual Property Office, the European Investment Bank, the new Unified Patent Court, and a range of research programmes like Natura2000, Horizon 20/20, ITER and Galileo, as well as educational exchange programmes like Erasmus+, Comenius, Socrates and others.[7] Simultaneous applications to these agencies and programmes will confirm that the UK wishes to remain a good neighbour to the EU, and might even spread a degree of goodwill. Will many members remain quite so determined to punish the UK, if it is simultaneously expressing its willingness to co-operate with the Intellectual Property Office or Horizon 20/20 or the EU's Common Foreign and Security Policy?

Agreements about these agencies and programmes and other multiple other relationships between the UK and the EU can be negotiated at a different pace and temperature than that of a trade agreement. If they are concluded after the UK no longer has any MEPs, or a UKREP office, and stopped making an annual contribution to the EU budget, is of little consequence. The EU has many such negotiations with third countries, which is what the UK by then will be.

Migration, a one-issue negotiation

Since the UK is not seeking to remain a member of the Single Market, it is difficult to see why migration should figure, even indirectly, in the trade negotiations. The only aspect of migration that remains to be negotiated is the guarantees to be given to current EU residents in the UK and current UK residents in the EU. This could and should be done, as the Prime Minister said, before the trade negotiations even begin, though it is not quite as non-contentious as many assumed, given the relevance of 'acquired rights' under the Vienna Convention and the European Convention on Human Rights.[8]

When she raised the issue at a meeting of the European Council in December, Mrs May was greeted with a stony silence.[9] In her January speech on withdrawal, she observed: 'I have told other EU leaders that we could give people the certainty they want straight away, and reach such a deal now. Many of them favour such an agreement – one or two others do not.' Identifying the one or two, so their citizens in the UK know who they are, might move things along. Or better, they might take the high ground, and give guarantees to all EU residents, before receiving those for UK expatriates in the EU. This might shame the EU into reciprocating, and incidentally demonstrate to Remainers that Brexit is not, as some of them believe, inherently xenophobic and racist, but simply committed to managed immigration.

In any event, once an agreement is reached on this, there is nothing left to argue about. As a matter of courtesy, the UK will no doubt, describe its new immigration rules, which will be non-discriminatory and apply equally to EU and non-EU citizens. Whatever their final form, they will seek to link the number of immigrants to available employment in the UK, probably by limiting resident visas to those in, or offered, employment, and cutting the number who arrive 'looking for work'. There were 105,000 of these in the year ending June 2016, 81,000 of whom were from the EU.[10] The new rules will no doubt include special visa provisions for intra-company transfers, students and seasonal agricultural workers. Since the UK has no reason or wish to restrict the number of skilled or unskilled immigrants from the EU with employment or a job offer in the UK, negotiations would only begin if the EU were unwilling to make the same offer to UK immigrants.[11]

These new immigration rules will, however, make an important contribution to the domestic debate about Brexit, and indirectly assist the negotiations. If they show, as expected, that they will not curtail UK firms' freedom to recruit employees from the EU or anywhere else when there is inadequate supply of suitable employees in the UK, they will dispel one of the anxieties of British employers.[12] If they are defined in advance of the negotiations, perhaps alongside the Great Repeal Bill, then two of the major sources of uncertainty will have been removed, which is a decided plus for the economy, and for UK negotiators.

A slimline exit trade agreement

As a result of the decision to withdraw from the Single Market, and after the passage of a comprehensive Great Repeal Bill, the trade agreement on withdrawal will necessarily be a slimline document as trade agreements go. It will include a tariff schedule of the EU's proposed tariffs and the UK's matching responses, and the barriers to services that have been clarified or amended. Like most trade agreements, the terms it sets may be phased in over several years, giving both parties time to adjust to the new rules and rates without disruptive overnight changes.

A new method of adjudication in the event of disputes will also be required, though that might perhaps be lifted from that CETA or T-TIP.[13] An agreement with these basic elements would allow trade between the two parties to continue, on a new legal footing, and with more paperwork and formalities, but otherwise relatively undisturbed. Why should it take more than the 18 months that M. Barnier anticipated?

Appendix I

Comments on *HM Treasury analysis: the long-term economic impact of EU membership and the alternatives*

- The Treasury model, like the academic studies it cited, referred to the trade of the EEC/EU *as a whole*, as it grew from nine to 28 members, but the Treasury went on to base estimates and predictions about the UK alone from these collective figures, despite the fact its own earlier 2005 study had found that trade between EU member states as a whole had been boosted by more than twice as much UK trade with them, and despite the fact that an OECD study cited by the Treasury had drawn attention to the 'sharp rise' in trade intensity of the eastern EU and 'quite stable' trade intensity of the western EU.[1]

- The Treasury claimed that 'the impact of EU membership on goods trade post-1987 is approximately double that of the pre-1987 impact ... [and] that the trade benefits from EU membership increase over time, suggesting the estimates used may underestimate the overall impact of EU membership'. To make such a claim without distinguishing the impact of the addition of 11 post-socialist states, and explaining how this has been discounted in this claim is unacceptable.[2]

- Like the studies it cites, the Treasury conflates the Common Market decades from 1973 to 1992, with well-documented high UK export growth, with the Single Market decades from 1993 to 2015, whose slow and declining export growth is equally well-documented.[3]

- The UK's deficit in the balance of payments for goods with the EU indicates that the growth of imports and exports differs, and its surplus in services shows that goods and services also differ. Bundling them all together was to opt, for no good reason, for a crude and clumsy total figure that gave a misleading picture of the impact of EU membership for referendum voters, and is unhelpful to the present debate about the best form of Brexit.

- In their brief references to three academic studies they give the impression that there is a settled consensus about the methodology and the estimates of such studies. Had they quoted these studies more fully, as will be shown below, or quoted other studies which disagree more widely from their own, they would have shown their readers that gravity model estimates were prone to enormously wide swings, from positive to negative, dependent on the inclusion or omission or proxy of one or two variables, and also have had to tell them that several studies have found that the impact of the EU on trade was nil or even negative.[4]

- Whilst it may be formally correct to say that the academic studies estimating that EEC/EU membership have boosted trade by between 50 per cent and 104 per cent are 'consistent with' the Treasury's own estimate of 75 per cent, in the sense that both are positive, most non-econometricians would find the spread of 50 per cent plus between these estimates disconcerting, and a reason for second thoughts, rather than reassuring.

- Moreover since these studies refer to goods trade, the Treasury should have pointed out that its estimate of a 75 per cent boost to trade referred to goods and services, while its own its estimate of the boost to goods trade alone was 115 per cent. It was therefore the outlier versus the studies it cites, not reassuringly in the midst of them.

- The frailty, and volatility, of such estimates is illustrated by the Treasury's own attempt to measure the impact of EEA membership on intra-EU services trade, a rather important question when debating the best Brexit option. They were surprised to find that the impact is 'unexpectedly large and negative, implying a fall in services trade with the EU of approximately 9 per cent'. They then decided to ignore this finding.[5] Advocates of EEA entry and a soft Brexit might be best advised to follow their example.

- On a previous occasion the Treasury relied on a gravity model which persuaded Gordon Brown to tell the Commons in 2003 that the UK government was in favour in principle of joining the euro, though at some later point in time.[6] The main author of the work on which the Treasury relied at that time, Andrew Rose, along with a frequent co-author, published a mea culpa in 2015, in which he admitted that after studying 15 years of EMU trade data 'we find no consistent evidence that EMU stimulated trade... Indeed (by one of our methodologies) the net effect of EMU on exports is negative.' Still more importantly, they decided that 'econometric methodology matters so much that it undermines confidence in our ability to estimate the effect of currency union on trade.'[7] One would expect, on such an important matter for the British people, the Treasury to explain why we should expect better results from the gravity model this time around, and why they felt able to overlook the problems of the econometric methodology that worried two of its major proponents. The Treasury felt under no such obligation. They simply ignored this bombshell.[8]

A note on the Treasury's selective and misleading citation of three academic studies

The Treasury claimed that 'academic research overwhelmingly concludes that EU membership has had a significant positive impact on trade flows between member states'.

This note lists the three academic studies mentioned, the most recent first, gives the Treasury's citation of the study, followed by a brief account of the content of the research, as far as possible in the author's own words. None of these studies make any reference to the UK. Hence in addition to the problems their authors describe, they also involve the additional risk of generalising from the collections of countries to the unique circumstances of the UK.

1. HMT citation: 'uses data from 1970 to 1995 for 196 countries and find that EU membership increases bilateral trade by 51 per cent'

Theo S. Eicher et al, 'Trade creation and diversion revisited: Accounting for model uncertainty and natural trading partner effects', *Journal of Applied Econometrics*. 27: 296–321 (2012), Published online 24 June 2010 in Wiley Online Library (wileyonlinelibrary. com) DOI: 10.1002/jae.1198

This paper addresses the uncertainty across the entire subject area of modelling the impact of trade agreements on trade flows. The theoretical literature suggests, it says, 'diverse and even contradictory' effects, while empirical research has produced 'remarkably disparate' results which the authors hope to resolve by introducing a new statistical technique into the empirical investigations. Their own investigation produces 'one surprise' in that it turns up an 'implied negative net trade creation for the EU'. They spend some time trying to explain, or explain away, this finding and other studies that have found 'similar negative EU results'. The paper ends by finding that the trade creation effects of the EU are at least positive, though its last word on the EU, as distinct from the other EIAs (economic integration agreements) is far from reassuring. 'The EU which oscillated from negative to positive coefficients is now economically significant, but only marginally statistically significant.' The Treasury might have quoted this sentence in its report.

2. HMT citation – 'uses data for 96 countries from 1960 to 2000 and find that EU membership increases intra-EU trade by over 90 per cent'

Scott L Baier et al, 'Do economic integration agreements actually work? Issues in understanding the causes and consequences of the growth of regionalism', pp. 461-497, *The world economy*, Vol.

31:4, 2008, http://onlinelibrary.wiley.com/wol1/doi/10.1111/j.1467-9701.2008.01092.x/full

Their first aim was 'to try to estimate with precision (and robustness) the ex post effects of various western European trade agreements on members' international trade', accounting for the endogeneity of trade agreements' formation. Their second aim was 'to establish that the economic effects of trade agreements on members' trade were much larger than previous estimates have suggested', which will, they think, 'help to explain the proliferation of trade agreements in later years'.

These twin aims sit rather uncomfortably beside one another, the first being a straightforward investigation discounting for endogeneity, that is, the tendency of countries to conclude agreements with partners with whom they already have considerable and growing trade. The second was to show that policy makers have acted rationally in concluding EIAs which include free trade agreements, even though ex ante studies predict only modest gains, and many *ex post* studies show that they had no impact on trade at all, or even a negative impact. They therefore set out to find a measure showing that the real impact was much greater.

They reviewed and progressively amend various techniques for measuring the impact of trade agreements and dismiss those that suggest agreements have limited or negative impact, on what grounds is not clear, except that they are not the results they are searching for. Estimates from 'a typical gravity equation specification' for instance 'are not very supportive that EIAs actually work', while estimates 'from the theoretically-motivated gravity equation using country fixed effects lend even less support to the notion that ex post EIAs actually work ... Some studies showed that membership in various stages of the EEC/EC/EU had a statistically significant negative effect on members' trade, as did the EEA's EU–EFTA free trade agreements. Such results seem implausible.' They therefore move on.

They eventually find what they are looking for, so the paper has a happy ending. 'Adjusting for unobserved time-invariant heterogeneity using bilateral fixed effects has a notable impact on the results' and shows that 'the vast bulk of EIAs have tended to augment members' trade by about 100 per cent over a 15-year period.' They rest content with this conclusion because it 'is consistent with anecdotal evidence from policy makers that the economic benefits from EIAs are much larger than conventional ex ante economic analyses have previously suggested'.

Whether the rest of us can be happy with the dismissal of other findings because they are, for some undisclosed reason 'implausible', and should also rest content because their final estimate is 'consistent with anecdotal evidence from policy makers', is not clear. In effect, they are using anecdotal evidence from policymakers to validate the methodology by which trade agreements are measured.

3. HMT citation – 'uses bilateral trade data for 130 countries from 1962 to 1996 to examine the ex-post impact of FTAs on trade flows. Their results suggest EU membership increased intra-EU trade by an average of 104 per cent over the period.'

Céline Carrere, 'Revisiting the effects of regional trade agreements on trade flows with proper specification of the gravity model', pp. 223-247, *Economic Review*, vol. 50, no. 2,. 2006. http://publi.cerdi. org/ed/2003/2003.10.pdf

Carrere examines the EU and six other trade agreements to show that studies using the panel method of estimation were 'more plausible' than those using cross sectional method. The former s howed that EU trade is 104 per cent above what is expected by other indicators (but for the years 1962 to 1996), while the latter estimated it is 21 per cent below.

The Treasury cited the former estimates of course, but failed to add that this method also found 'significant' trade diversion of imports and exports. 'In general, the findings of this study, covering seven RTAs, show that most of these RTAs resulted in an increase in intra-regional trade beyond levels predicted by the gravity model, often coupled with a reduction in imports from the rest of the world, and at times coupled with a reduction in exports to the rest of the world, suggesting evidence of trade diversion'.

The Treasury most probably forgot this qualification because later in its analysis it argued that there were no trade diversion effects and that 'membership of the Single Market gives the EU an important role in facilitating access to non-EU markets'.

Appendix II

On the role of trade associations in a post-Brexit trade intelligence network

Key witnesses that went missing

As will be clear from the main text, one of the main disappointments for anyone collecting evidence about the benefits of the Single Market, in order to make an informed choice about the best Brexit option for the UK, is the absence of reliable and systematic information from trade associations about the sectors in which their members operate.

Their reluctance to collect, analyse and publish data which would enable the merits of the Single Market and of EU trade agreements for their sector to be evaluated was strikingly evident in the Trade and Investment submissions to the Balance of Competences Review in 2013. Most of the 38 submissions enthusiastically supported EU membership and its trade agreements, some with qualifications, but none presented or cited trustworthy research to support their conclusions, even though they had been invited to do so by the FCO when initiating the review.

Trade associations were also noticeable absentees from the referendum debate, despite some media interviews, press releases and funds to support Remain, the detailed data of the kind that they were in the best position to collect, showing the benefits of the Single Market for their sectors, and the disadvantages of trading under WTO rules, was missing.

As far as one tell, they seem likely to continue to maintain their silence during the debate about the best Brexit option. TheCityUK commissioned a report that supplied useful evidence that had been missing from the referendum debate about financial services.[1] Otherwise, we have had to depend on a CBI report which conveyed the worries of some unknown number of their members, sector by sector, but gave no data to enable one to judge whether a sector was especially dependent on the benefits of the Single Market, or deserved special attention in the negotiations, or whether they were merely voicing understandable, pervasive concern about the uncertainties of the Brexit process.[2] It is difficult to believe that this will be of any greater use to the UK negotiators than its pre-referendum report was to intelligent voters.

For a number of reasons, the absence of detailed and telling evidence from trade associations about their own sectors is surprising, since they have certain in-built advantages when collecting data from their own sectors. Member companies probably give state agencies no more information than they are legally required to give, are not likely to give much information about performance in specific markets to shareholders in their annual reports, and will naturally be wary of giving data that might prove embarrassing, or market sensitive, or helpful to competitors, to researchers or journalists with whom they have no continuing relationship.

One expects them to be more forthcoming to their own trade associations. Membership is voluntary, usually permanent, and often combines official functions with social occasions. Members know their association exists to defend their interests as a sector or an industry, and must collect information if they are to do this effectively. One therefore imagines that their members will be especially co-operative, knowing that their anonymity will be preserved if they request it, and that trade associations would therefore provide the most insightful and persuasive analyses of the impact of the Single Market, and of the EU's trade agreements.

They never did so, or if they did, their work remains unpublished. Perhaps they are now providing UK negotiators with reliable and insightful insider evidence. Outside observers, hoping to form a view of the best Brexit option will have to make do without it.

After Brexit, however, when the UK has to define its own trade policy and negotiate its own trade agreements, the unresearched impressions of members' views, of the kind submitted to the FCO, supplemented by private exchanges with policy-makers, will fall far short of what the UK will require in the wholly new post-Brexit trading environment. In this new environment, trade associations will have to play a more significant and proactive role than they have during the years of EU membership, ever since responsibility for devising trade policy, and settling the priorities in trade negotiations, was passed to Brussels.

The debilitating legacy of EU membership

Before trying to define the new post-Brexit role of trade associations, it may be as well to consider how their current behaviour may have been shaped by 43 years of EU membership. From the beginning, it has meant the transposition of directives and imposition of regulations, on an increasingly large range of issues, most especially during the 23 years of the Single Market. Trade associations, or the larger ones at least, might try to influence or tweak these regulations before they came into force, seeking the help of kindred associations in other member countries as well as UK MEPs and UKREP. But their primary tasks were keeping track of the proposed regulation through the complex EU 'legislative' process and, at the end, analysing the approved directive or regulation and explaining its probable consequences for their members. Given the sheer quantity of regulation needed to create the level playing field of the Single Market, these tasks must have defined their role over all the years of membership.

What clearly was not so important was influencing and evaluating the trade strategy of the Commission. It is sometimes claimed that the UK had a disproportionate influence on the EU's trade policy, and noted that it has had more trade commissioners than any other member country (four: Soames, Brittan, Mandelson, and Ashton). This is, however, hardly an illuminating measure, since they were bound by oath not to represent or promote British interests. In any case, for many years external trade was not itself a primary concern of the EU. Trade agreements were a substitute for an EU foreign policy before it had the treaty-defined right to have such a thing. They were therefore used to maintain friendly relationships with the former colonies of member countries and neighbouring countries and often included an element of foreign aid. They also had a number of other worthy goals such as exporting European values, upholding and extending human and gender rights in the partner country, and contributing to the fight against climate change.

Increasing trade was therefore but one concern among many, and it seems doubtful that trade associations could have been especially interested, or influential in contributing to this kind of trade policy. The agreements themselves tell the story. They collectively covered a tiny proportion of UK world trade outside Europe. The idea that these reflected UK preferences, or were strongly influenced by the UK, or that UK trade associations helped to shape them, is patently absurd.

Moreover, for many years the European Commission declined to discover whether its agreements had in fact increased trade at all. It would commission *ex ante* 'sustainability impact assessments' to make the case for the agreement, but only in recent years has it begun to commission *ex post* assessments, and thus far has completed only one, which says not a word about its impact on the UK. The UK governments, like other member governments, evidently believed that membership relieved them of any responsibility of evaluating the impact of the trade agreements, and trade associations seem to have followed suit, and declined to conduct any *ex post* impact assessments of their own. The Commission therefore remained totally unaccountable for its trade policy and its agreements, though given their mixed goals it might have been difficult in any event to decide how that might best be done. It didn't matter. Without having made the least effort to discover whether they had helped to increase UK trade with the partner countries or not, the CBI and many UK trade associations were ready in 2013 to enthusiastically commend the EU's trade agreements.

The legacy from the years of EU membership is therefore an unfortunate and debilitating one. The Commission adopted a trade agreement strategy without any forward intelligence on trade prospects and goals, conducted sustainability impact assessments of the selected partner but not a trade one, negotiated with mixed motives, did not subsequently conduct research to assess the impact of its agreements, and has never been held to account by anyone, but was nonetheless warmly applauded. Clearly, there is nothing positive for post-Brexit UK to learn from this EU experience. It constitutes a wholly negative reference model, illustrating almost everything the new Department of International Trade should not do.

It is no less a negative model for trade associations. Along with large multinationals, some of the largest associations appear to have been able to lobby successfully, but most appear to have been little more than passive observers. Judging by the submissions to the Balance of Competence Review, the only other function they performed was to lodge complaints about the behaviour of some trade partner with the Commission and then hope the Commission would process it through the appropriate channels, if need be to a WTO dispute panel. They were certainly not invited or expected to conduct any research about any past or future EU trade agreements, or of course about the Single Market itself.

Of the dozens of submissions to the Balance of Competences Review only one, the Society of Motor Manufacturers & Traders (SMMT), grasped the essential role that research must play in devising an effective trade policy. It put the case in a nutshell:

> A key principle for SMMT is using sound economic analysis for determining which markets the EU should pursue trade agreements with. The role of UK government should be in advising and communicating its trade priorities to actors at a European level, based on a transparent method of economic assessment in determining key strategic trade partners. Within government's economic assessment of key trading partners' growth markets and sectors with comparative advantage, particular attention should be put on those markets where there is significant future potential to export.[3]

When this was written the UK was not only still a member of the EU, it was not thinking of leaving it. It says much about attitudes at the time that even such a large and influential association as the SMMT thought it appropriate to defer to the Government to conduct research rather than to do it themselves. Little did it realise, that the Government was itself deferring to the European Commission, and had not been conducting any such research since it had entered the EEC. The UK had, it seems, not only surrendered the right to negotiate its own trade agreements, but also willingly surrendered the right to conduct its own investigations about the merits of the trade policies on which their exporters now depended, and that same attitude somehow seems to have spread to trade associations directly involved. It is as if EU membership absolved everyone of any responsibility, and individual exporters were left to trade as best they might. If such attitudes were to continue after Brexit, the UK's already poor export performance could hardly be expected to improve.

Their role in a post-Brexit trade intelligence network

The first step by which trade associations can define and assume a role, suited to the post-Brexit environment, is to obtain from all their member companies the HS 6 digit codes of the products they export, and to which countries. Associations that already possess these codes will find the role change relatively easy, since they will already have realised that these codes are the primary means by which they can effectively assist their members in world markets. Those who do not know them should take it as indication that they are currently less than fully capable of helping members improve their export performance. Only when they have them, will they be able to advise their members of the specific world markets that present their best opportunities, make informed judgements about the best trade promotion events and locations, for themselves or UKTI, and contribute to the negotiation and revision of future UK trade agreements that will best help their members.

With the six digits of these codes, associations can refer, on their members' behalf, to the basic Trade Map database provided on the website of the Geneva-based International Trade Centre. This will enable them to compare the markets in which their members currently trade with a world marketplace of 220 countries and territories.

Among other things, it provides a regularly updated record enabling them:

- To see the value of UK exports of their products, as a percentage of world exports, as a percentage of exports in their HS sectors in up to 220 of individual markets, though a few are missing, with UK trade surpluses or deficits in those markets.

- To see the growth of their members' exports since 2001 vs the growth of world exports, vs competing exporters, in specific markets.

- To compare the specific markets in which they compete effectively with exporters of their products from identified other countries by comparison with those in which they do not.

- To identify, quite quickly, discrepancies and anomalies in their members' export performance that is to say when it does not admit of any straightforward explanation in terms of an exchange rates, or a tariff differential or competitors' trade agreement or proximity to the market, or product quality.

- To identify some of the peculiarities of every export market, as well as the importers of their products in every country, by name, firm size and turnover, by website, email address, etc.

- To conduct intensive analysis of bilateral trade relationships showing who exports what, to where, at what rate of growth, for a period covering the past 15 years.

For the present, the Trade Map does not provide anything like the same level of information about services, so service trade associations will have, for the time being at least, to generate their own equivalent data sources.

Here is an example of how a quick search of this website to identify issues can be undertaken.

A four-click illustration of the use of the ITC Trade Map to formulate an evidence-based trade policy.

The first click is simply to get the most general view of UK exports from the point of view of a policy analyst or policy-maker who is interested in the problem of the relatively low rate of growth of UK goods exports, and its chronic goods trade deficit, and wishes to know what might be done about it.

Since we cannot look at all UK goods exports at once, we have chosen the top 10 in value in 2015, categorised by their HS chapter or two-digit number. The data about them is presented in Figure A2.1 in the form of export growth matrices. The size of the bubbles on the chart, corresponding to their total value, and the colour indicating whether they earned a surplus (blue) or a deficit when the UK imported more than it exported (yellow). The vertical position of the bubble shows whether the products in each sector have kept pace with world import demand or not. If they are above the horizontal red line, showing that world import growth in 2015 fell by two per cent, they have, and if they are below it, they haven't.

These are the UK top 10 exports in value, so most of them are, not surprisingly perhaps, above it. There is just one dazzling performer, '88 – aircraft, spacecraft and parts thereof', which is all but alone in the top right-hand quadrant showing 'winners in growing sectors' with a 100 percentage increase in its share of world exports over the five years from 2011 to 2015. This is where the policymaker wants every sector to be, but most straddle the boundary between this quadrant and the top left-hand quadrant 'losers in growing sectors', meaning their share of world exports has remained about the same over these years.

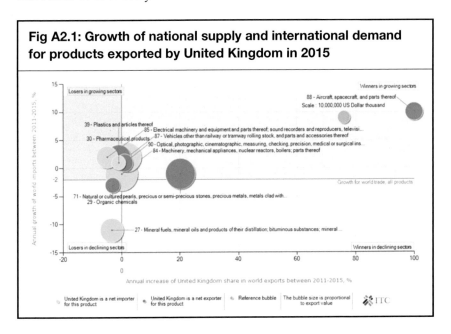

Fig A2.1: Growth of national supply and international demand for products exported by United Kingdom in 2015

The horizontal position of the bubble indicates the growth in the sectors' contribution to the UK share of world exports in 2015. Again 88 is the star performer, with the much larger '71 – Natural or cultured pearls, precious metals...' doing quite well, and all the others clustering around the vertical red line showing little or no change.

More detailed information about each of these sectors is available by clicking each button. However, to get much more detail, and closer so to speak to the front line, it is better to expand HS sector to four digits. To show how to breakdown the sectors into more detail, we have chosen at random HS 90. It is shown in Figure A2.2 in the same growth matrix, though only the top ten four digits of HS 90 are given, simply to give an uncluttered view.

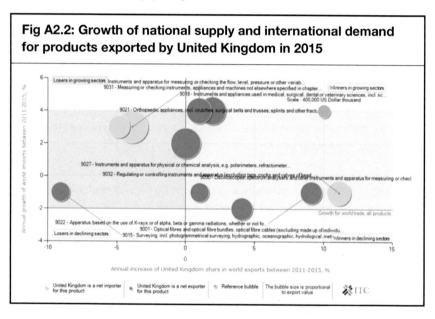

Fig A2.2: Growth of national supply and international demand for products exported by United Kingdom in 2015

In the first click HS 90 seemed a rather average performer in growth terms, though with a trade surplus, but with 4 digits we can that this sector contains both winners and losers, with rather more in the 'winners in growing sectors' quadrant. However, there is one quite striking 'loser in a growing sector' and that is 9015. It is striking because it earns a trade surplus, and might therefore feel quite proud of itself, but in terms of growth, and of the growth of UK share in world exports, it is performing rather badly. So to understand what is happening, and to explore 9015 future prospects a little further, we make a third click to identify the markets in which it is failing to grow.

The matrix shown in Figure A2.3 identifies them, again limiting the number of markets on the chart to 20 for the sake of clarity. It is important to note that the colours of the bubbles here do not refer to the trade balance, but to whether the UK exports to that market have been growing more than that markets total imports of the product, blue if they have, and yellow if they haven't. If the bubble is in a high position on the chart, it means it is a high growth market, so a high bubble in yellow means, a fast growing market in which UK exports are not keeping pace with the growth, and the bigger the bubble of course, the greater the missed opportunity, and the more worthy of the policy-makers' attention. There are a fair number yellow bubbles and some of them are quite far above the red line showing the world growth of imports of 9015 over the five years from 2011 to 2015.

Fig A2.3: Growth in demand for a product exported by United Kingdom in 2015. Product: 9015 Surveying, incl. photogrammetrical surveying, hydrographic, oceanographic, hydrological, meteorological or geophysical instruments and appliances (excluding compasses); rangefinders

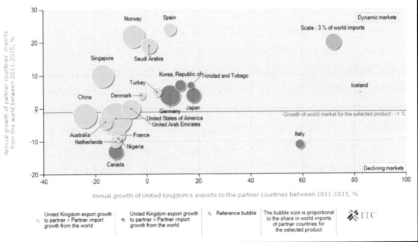

To get further details, and to give further thought to, the performance shown in the chart, we might click the bubbles of interest, but instead we will use our fourth click to switch to a more traditional table to see the actual figures over the five years.

When we do this, the table is more extensive than can be reproduced on a single page. A small part of it is reproduced in Table A2.1, including only the 20 countries in the Figure A2.3, leaving behind 175 small and tiny markets and dropping seven variables which seemed of lesser, though not insignificant, analytical leverage.

Sector HS 9015 had, as we have already seen, a good export performance over the years from 2011 to 2015, in the sense that it has a trade surplus overall, and in many of its largest markets. These figures show, what was not clear before, that the UK is the second largest exporter of these products in the world, after the United States.

Apart from the US, the deficits are, oddly enough, all with fellow Single Market countries, and this continues beyond the table. Austria and Finland are the other notable deficit countries in the smaller markets. Why the Single Market should be distinctive in this manner is a mystery, like many others in the main text, and equally worthy of further investigation, with some help perhaps from an insider informant in the trade association or the companies involved.

However, we also saw in the earlier matrix that the sector was in the 'loser in growing sectors' quadrant, and the figures in this table explain how it earned this status. The value of its exports to the world, from 2011 to 2015, fell by 10 per cent, whereas world imports of these products fell by only 1 per cent. This pattern is repeated in the majority of the 20 partner countries listed here. The growth UK's exports to Norway from 2011 to 2015 (5 per cent) has not kept pace with Norway's total demand for these products (22 per cent) over the same period. Over the five years there are only seven countries where the growth in the value of UK exports has exceeded that of the growth in the total value of the imports of HS 9015 in that market: Italy, Canada, Japan, Korea, Germany, Iceland, and Trinidad and Tobago.

Table A2.1: List of importing markets for the product [HS 9015] exported by United Kingdom in 2015

Surveying, incl. photogrammetrical surveying, hydrographic, oceanographic , hydrological, meteorological or geophysical instruments and appliances (excluding compasses); rangefinders. United Kingdom's exports represent 9.3% of world exports for this product, its ranking in world exports is 2.

Importers	Value exported in 2015 (USD thousand)	Trade balance 2015 (USD thousand)	Share in United Kingdom's exports (%)	Growth in exported value between 2011-2015 (%, p.a.)	Total imports growth in value of partner countries between 2011-2015 (%, p.a.)	Average tariff (estimated) faced by United Kingdom (%)
World	855075	285706	100	-10	-1	
Norway	173911	139581	20.3	-5	22	0
United States	144309	-25626	16.9	-12	-3	1.1
Un'td Arab Emirates	39816	38120	4.7	-6	0	5
Singapore	28229	22903	3.3	-17	10	
Italy	27254	25419	3.2	59	-11	0
Japan	23777	9490	2.8	18	4	0
Saudi Arabia	23478	23191	2.7	1	19	5
China	22112	3817	2.6	-24	-2	6
Canada	20618	7038	2.4	-12	-13	1.5
Korea, Rep	18085	16840	2.1	13	7	0
Netherlands	17728	-11509	2.1	-12	-10	0
Germany	17641	-66146	2.1	9	4	0
France	17133	-14776	2	-11	-8	0
Denmark	16820	13671	2	-2	4	0
Iceland	16154	14244	1.9	82	5	0
Nigeria	13639	12790	1.6	-11	-9	5
Trinidad & Tobago	13079	10768	1.5	17	7	0
Turkey	12821	11537	1.5	4	5	
Spain	12249	-703	1.4	9	24	0
Australia	10153	5682	1.2	-16	-4	0

Source: ITC calculations based on UN COMTRADE statistics

The biggest discrepancies between UK export growth and partner country's import growth (with the percentage difference) are found in Norway (-27), Singapore (-27), China (-22) Saudi Arabia (-18) and Spain (-13). Two of these have a tariff barrier. Three of these also happen to be the fastest growing markets for these products: Spain, Norway, and Saudi Arabia – in that order.

Thus, we have been able to initially identify opportunities that UK exporters of these products appear to have missed, though one would be wary of drawing conclusions from a two-minute search. It would be advisable to conduct a further search of the HS six digit code, speak to the exporters named therein, and/or their trade association, check the figures over a longer time period, (ITC data starts from 2001) and also try to understand why the direct data of this table does not square with the mirror data.[4]

However, we have delimited and mapped one promising area meriting further investigation both for those at national policy level hoping to address the UK chronic balance of trade deficit. And for the benefit of trade association in that sector, we can and will go further to six digits, identify by name the UK exporters to markets growing at a faster pace than their exports, as well as the names of the importers in those markets, and the names of their more successful competitors.

It may be of interest to discover what countries' exporters have been gaining in the markets in which the growth of UK exports has declined. China will serve as an example since UK exports to it declined by 22 per cent more than its imports increased. China is the world's second largest importer of HS 9015 products, after the United States, though over these five years its imports declined by 2 per cent, which is 1 per cent more than the world average. It also has the highest tariff of world importers, 6 per cent. While UK exports to China declined by 24 per cent, Chinese imports from Norway increased by 31 per cent, from Germany by 12 per cent, from Finland by 11 per cent and from Singapore by 8 per cent.

And obviously with further clicks, it is possible to do the same with all the other growing markets, and to build a more comprehensive picture of the UK's world export performance in

9015 products, and hence make more intelligent decisions about who should do what, where, and when to improve it.

Trade associations' research role on behalf of their SME members

Large companies with competent export departments will already be using this database, perhaps with their own supplements or equivalents. However, trade associations reach the very large number of SMEs who may not have the time or resources to do so. Hence information drawn from it, supplied regularly to their members, with an informed sector-wide commentary which they are best qualified to provide, would enable SME members to evaluate their own performance versus their competitors worldwide, and to see where their best opportunities for export growth are to be found. Trade associations are the best, perhaps the only, organizations who could use research of this kind for the benefit of SMEs in world markets. It is far beyond the capacity of any government department or national agency, even one as specifically committed as UKTI. They could not possibly digest or understand the amount of hard and soft data involved, nor provide the continuing informed commentary and research, to influence and guide SMEs.

After examining the basic data in the ITC Trade Map or some equivalent source, the next task of the association is to decide, in consultation with their own members, how their observed market failures may be best explained. Whether tariff and non-tariff barriers might be responsible, or trade agreements that help their competitors, or product quality, or ineffective distribution or local marketing and advertising. However, if they can dismiss these usual suspects, the database can help to identify what might be called puzzling or discrepant or anomalous performances in export markets. Theses come in various forms, such as poor performance in some markets that does not square with effective performance in others, when exporters of a given product to some partner countries ignore others known to import that same product in significant quantities, or when similar member companies export successfully and others remain in the UK domestic market.

Research has, in short, to become a central function of the post-Brexit trade association. It has to become the well- informed but critical interrogator of its own members, setting export standards and targets, examining on their behalf world markets which raise questions, conducting or commissioning further research, getting expert help when required from the partner country, such as the local office of the Department of International Trade, or the partner country's Chamber of Commerce. Associations are better placed than individual SMEs to perform these functions.

International trade department staff

The precise relationship between the new Department of International Trade (DIT) and the Foreign Office has still to be settled and institutionalised, but we may assume that the new Department of International Trade will be primarily responsible analysing UK world trade, identifying its present weaknesses, recommending remedies, both to those directly involved, and in terms of government policy. The latter includes the amendment of existing trade agreements to which the UK has been committed as a member of the EU, and more importantly the negotiation of new agreements.

This department will require an appropriately skilled career staff, single-mindedly committed to extending UK export markets, some of whom will be located in the UK's major partner countries. It will be regularly held accountable for its priorities and policies, for its chosen form of support and intervention, and wherever possible, by its impact on UK export growth. It follows that such a department will be the first and regular point of contact for trade associations with exporting members and individual exporting companies. To have informed exchanges with them both, it follows that it too will need to know the HS six digit codes of every UK exporter, as well as the countries to which they are currently exported.

The compilation of such a directory is not the daunting task that it may seem at first sight, since it can be done in conjunction with trade associations, with the ITC Trade Map, and with commercial trade directories. In any event, it cannot be shirked or postponed since it is the foundation of an effective post-Brexit trade policy. In the days when the UK conducted its own trade policy, it appears to have been a somewhat blunt and diffuse instrument never knowing for sure where incentives or pressures might be best applied. Trade promotion continues in the same rather ill focussed manner today, selling the UK in general with no one really knowing whether trade fairs and exhibitions, 'British weeks', promotion events, or royal and prime ministerial visits, are happening in the right markets, or have any lasting impact.

Information technology, and the groundwork of ITC, makes it possible to focus precisely on particular markets in specific countries, and to measure the impact of such efforts. Brexit makes it essential to do so. Staff posted to partner countries will therefore have, on landing, a regularly updated record of the partner economy's demand for imports in relevant sectors, the nature of those particular sub-markets, the identity of its main importers, along with the names and email addresses of UK exporters to those markets. They will also be able to compare the UK's main competitors in the same sectors, and to target their attention and advice on those UK firms and trade associations most likely to benefit from it.

The enlarged participation of universities

Establishing links between the locally-based staff of the Department of International Trade and trade associations and their members is a critical part of the formation of a new Trade Intelligence Network, but universities will also be key participants.

Some UK universities have already played a small part in EU trade policy, by commissioning research, usually to conduct *ex ante* sustainability impact assessments mentioned above, or other *ad hoc* research. As the UK comes to define and amending its own trade relationships worldwide, their participation will be required on a more significant scale.

To begin with, university economics departments will have to expand and create new programmes to provide appropriate skills in the analysis of international trade for those entering the many new careers in the public and private sectors that will necessarily be created, both at home and abroad, in DIT, in trade associations, and in the export departments of larger firms.

Moreover, research will be required to help DIT decide the UK's negotiating priorities, both in selecting partner countries, and in substance of the agreements, whether amending existing EU agreements or embarking on new bilateral agreements. Since the UK has the opportunity break with the very bad practice of the European Commission, it should also routinely produce ex post impact assessments of the trade agreements to which it is committed, starting with those it has inherited from the EU, and in due course including those it has negotiated independently. Brexit means the end of the era of the unaccountable trade policy.

Maybe trade associations ought to change, but how can they be persuaded to do so?

It would be unreasonable to suppose that all UK trade associations will spontaneously recognise that Brexit requires them to change their role and assume research tasks that they previously left to the Government, or to the European Commission, or to their own members. What kind of incentives and pressures might encourage them to do so?

The first is the appearance of a new interested and informed partner, the DIT, that is ready to exchange ideas, and to help them and their members adapt to exporting in the post-Brexit trading environment. In the first instance, the Department of International Trade will only be putting together a profile of their members' export performance and prospects. However, when it makes clear it can help to define the best market prospects in their sector and help members to achieve their targets, either with expert assistance in the UK, or by trade promotion, or by the input of their staff in foreign markets, it might encourage associations to invest time and effort in establishing a friendly working relationship.

The associations will also be aware that DIT will be negotiating over the next few years a series of new trade agreements, and that it expects trade associations to have a significant input on the substance of those agreements, no longer having to make themselves heard in the Brussels mêlée. This should be quite a strong incentive to maintain amiable, on-going working relationships with the Department, and to conduct the kind of research that will be needed to make a persuasive case on behalf of their members.

The responses of the Department International Trade to these reports, including those from the staff based in the target country, will define the character of this new relationship. It should be built around a shared commitment to export growth and the pursuit of realistic, specific evidence-based goals, rather than vague aspirations. Their exchanges will, incidentally, provide a running commentary on UK export performance, and provide a means by which both parties can be held accountable. They might also make the trade negotiators job a little easier by helping improve the effectiveness of future agreements, as well as conveying to the association and its members that their opinions matter, and they can directly, and routinely, influence trade policy. As EU members, that sentiment must have been limited to the very largest pan-Europe multinationals with permanent lobbyists and liaison staff in Brussels, and maybe a few of the largest trade associations. Those that spoke only for membership in a single country would inevitably have had rather few victories under their belt, and more often have had to accept that as one of 28, they would necessarily have to compromise or be overlooked much of the time.

The second way of pushing trade associations to redefine themselves as research bodies is to recognise, and perhaps reward, them as such in their tax returns. Providing members with regular analytics, of an appropriate standard, about their performance and goals in world markets might be made a defining status of associations that are recognised partners of DIT, and distinguished from those that prefer to continue with their traditional social, networking or trade promotion and PR functions. Their status might also be recognised when they need help from DIT staff in the markets that matter to them.

Appendix III

On the Scottish Government's puzzling enthusiasm for membership of the Single Market

Since the Scottish Government is a fervent enthusiast for continued membership of the Single Market, and thinks that a hard Brexit and trading under WTO rules 'would severely damage Scotland's economic, social and cultural interests' and 'will hit jobs and living standards – deeply and permanently', one not unnaturally expects to find evidence to support this emphatic stand in its formal presentation of its preferred Brexit options.[1]

One hopes, in particular, to see evidence of the benefits that Scotland has derived from the Single Market, showing how its exporters have grown in contrast with competitors who have been exporting to the EU under WTO rules. Perhaps some reference to whisky, which we know has gained little from either the Single Market or EU trade agreements, or to fishing, so that we might hear how it would answer the spokesmen of the Scottish industry who have enthusiastically supported both Brexit and withdrawal from the Single Market.[2]

These hopes are soon dashed. Neither whisky nor fishing, nor any other sectors are separately examined or mentioned in this policy statement. There is no evidence at all about Scotland's export performance in the Single Market except the familiar Remain argument that Scotland exports a lot (42 per cent of its total exports) to its 27 closest neighbours. This only tells us that Scotland is no different from every other country in the world. There is no comparative evidence about countries with which it trades under WTO rules in order to give us some idea of how hard Scotland might be hit when the UK leaves the Single Market.

There are predictions of possible future gains and losses of course. It claims that if the UK were to leave the Single Market it could cost the Scottish economy, according to 'a range of external organisations' which are not identified, 'up to around £11 billion per year'.[3] It also relies on a model-based estimate 'that the losses in bilateral trade with other EEA countries from leaving the European Single Market could be as much as 60 per cent'.[4]

Nothing more can be said about the claims of external organisations that are not identified, except that £11 billion per year is very close to the total value of Scotland's EU exports in 2014, so these 'external organisations' apparently think a total cessation of Scotland's EU trade is a possibility. Not much more need be said about predictions based on a similar model to that used by the Treasury to make various far-fetched claims discussed in the main text.[5] However, it acknowledges that the impact of withdrawal from the Single Market will vary across sectors, and says that the Scottish government 'are undertaking further analysis to assess the impact on specific sectors under different Brexit scenarios.' We must therefore look forward to them.

The paper raises the question why anyone hoping to discover the best Brexit option for the people of Scotland would start with highly speculative estimates derived from a model that has been thrown into doubt, while ignoring the evidence published by the Scottish Government itself about Scotland's export performance with the EU compared with countries under WTO rules.

This shows that Scotland's exports to the EU have been virtually static since 2002, growing by just 6 per cent, while the larger proportion of exports going to the rest of the world, the overwhelming majority of which we know are under WTO rules, have grown by 74 per cent. The largest proportion of its exports, to the rest of the UK, has grown by 69 per cent.[6] It is surely disconcerting to focus attention and concern on Scotland's relatively small and static exports to the Single Market, while ignoring the much larger and faster-growing exports to the rest of the world and to the UK.

Moreover, it is not clear that leaving the Single Market would do any harm to Scotland's major exports to the EU. We must wait, of course, for the promised sectoral analyses, but data already published in earlier Scottish Government sources suggest the impact would be slight.[7] The total value of all Scottish exports in 2014 was £27.5 billion, of which £11.56 billion (42 per cent) went to the EU. Its two most important exports were whisky and refined petroleum and chemical products, but the EU tariffs on whisky are zero, and on refined petroleum and chemical products are zero or very low.[8] Hence they notably suffer by leaving the Single Market and having to trade under WTO rules, except no doubt by increased paper work. Together these two exports were 43 percent of the value of all Scottish goods exports. If they were the same proportion of EU exports as of total exports, just under £5 billion of Scottish goods exports, at their 2014 value, would be at risk if EU trade were to be seriously at risk by leaving the Single Market and trading under WTO rules.[9]

Pending the publication of the sectoral analyses, we can identify one sector that would not present a serious problem, even though it would face the highest EU tariffs of all, namely Agriculture, Forestry and Fishing. Scottish exports of these goods to the EU in 2014 totalled a miniscule £42 million, which is 0.36 per cent of its total exports to the EU.

Scotland also exported services of £5.87 billion to the EU, but many of those cannot be at risk since we know that the single market in services barely exists, and that the exports of services to the EU of countries trading with it under WTO rules have grown faster than member countries exports to each other. So, there is no reason to think that they would be as hard hit as the Government claims. Financial and insurance services is the most vulnerable service sector and might be affected by the ending of passporting, should that happen with no equivalents being agreed. However, if financial and insurance services exports to the EU they were the same 11.1 per cent as they are of Scotland's total world services exports, this would put £0.65 billion of services exports to the EU at most risk when leaving the Single Market.

In total therefore, something under £5 billion of Scottish goods exports might be at risk, and some unknown proportion of its £5.87 billion of its services exports, though most likely £0.65 billion of financial services would be at risk when the UK leaves the Single Market. This is a rather small proportion of Scotland's total exports, with exports to the rest of the world at £15.2 billion and to the rest of the UK, which in 2014 were put, at the very least, at £48.5 billion.[10] The Scottish Government's claim, without having examined any of the costs of the Single Market, that there is an 'overwhelming' case, on trade grounds, for continued membership of it, is difficult to take seriously, though when they identify the sectors that they have reason to think will be seriously affected it may be worth more attention.[11]

Moreover, the determination shown in this statement to maintain its rather small and static trade with the EU, while treating its fast-growing and far larger trade with the rest of the world and the rest of the UK as a secondary concern, to be sorted in some manner, including perhaps an 'invisible border' with England after Scotland has remained in the Single Market, suggests this policy has not been evaluated by normal economic criteria, nor with regard to the best economic interests of the Scottish people.

There must be, one is forced to conclude, other grounds for demanding that Scotland remain in the Single Market, and the economic costs and benefits of Single Market membership for the Scottish people is not the main concern. Such economic evidence as there is in this paper is rather perfunctory, almost window dressing, as if the Scottish Government had made up its mind even before it has collected and examined relevant economic evidence. It seems to already know that its sectoral studies will confirm its firm stand, even before they have been completed.

In several ways, the text of this policy statement shows that the Scottish Government had other considerations in mind and was not primarily concerned with conducting a serious economic assessment of the costs and benefits of Single Market membership.

- First, there is, as mentioned, no assessment of the costs of the Single Market. Perhaps this was because none of the direct costs of EU membership appear on the books of the Scottish Government. Though none of the indirect costs, including the cost of the regulation of firms not engaged in international trade and the cost of trade lost due to the European Commission's dismal record in negotiating trade agreements, which is mentioned either, are included.[12] The reader is invited to think that membership costs nothing at all. Scotland has, it is true, been a net beneficiary of EU funds until recently, but Scottish taxpayers and businesses have started to make a net contribution. This is still, according to David Bell of the University of Stirling, significantly less than their English counterparts, but nonetheless no longer nil and along with the indirect costs they deserve some mention in any adequate assessment.[13]

- Second, the EU itself is portrayed as the source of funds for an extremely long list of public and private recipients of EU funding, many of them apparently being 'heavily reliant' on it.[14] By contrast with EU costs, many of these grants from the EU do appear on the Scottish Government's books. In the public sector, they have contributed to local infrastructure, to government fuel poverty programmes, to regional initiatives to support inclusive growth, to housing investment and in large amounts to universities. The private sector has received EU funding for agriculture of course, for fishing, for food and drink manufacturing, for superfast broadband, for clean, innovative technologies to explore ocean energy, alternative fuels, energy storage and smart grid technology, and for tidal energy and wind farms.

At no point, does this statement mention that all these grants, including those to universities, are in fact paid by the UK taxpayer, whose annual payments far exceed all the funding and grants received by Scotland and the rest of the UK.[15] The Scottish Government is therefore making a case for the Single Market to Scots who are still unaware that the UK taxpayer is their ultimate benefactor and who still imagine that the EU raises money from somewhere or other, which it then grants, for some reason, to worthy Scots recipients. This case cannot form part of any serious cost benefit analysis of Single Market membership.

- This policy statement is throughout extremely enthusiastic, and at times lyrical, about the economic and cultural benefits of free movement of persons for Scotland, and also for Scots who wish to work elsewhere in the EU.[16] No data is given for either group. And no thought is paid to other UK countries whose inward migration might have been running at less manageable levels than Scotland's. Less than 6 per cent of the current residents of Scotland are immigrants, while in England and Wales the proportion is just over nine per cent.[17] Immigrant density in Scotland is just four per sq km, while in England and Wales, which already have one of the highest population densities in the EU, it is 34.[18] Freedom of movement may incur costs elsewhere in the UK which may be ignored, since it apparently only has benefits for Scotland. From the Scottish Government point of view free movement is therefore another benefit of the Single Market without any costs worth considering, and leaving it would, the paper seems to imply, bring immigration to an end. Though of course the UK government has never suggested or implied any such thing.

- Finally, membership of the Single Market is essential less because of its economic benefits, which it hasn't bothered to calculate, and more because the EU is the source of all the rights that the Scottish people currently enjoy. Not only their right of free movement, since 'the rights and freedoms we enjoy as members of the European Single Market include the rights and interests of workers ... employment rights, social protection, equality rights, social inclusion and disability rights', as well as 'environmental and consumer rights', 'health and safety', and 'rights to equal treatment in to the context financial support for studies' and other unspecified 'human rights advances'.[19]

These rights are apparently safest in the hands of the European Commission, and of the six Scottish MEPs or maybe of the two from Scotland's governing party in Brussels.[20] In any event, on leaving the Single Market, they would become the responsibility of the Westminster Parliament, and therefore immediately be at risk, despite Scotland's 59 MPs. The Scottish Government would therefore expect substantial devolution if the UK were to leave the Single Market, so that these rights might be protected.[21]

In sum, according to the Scottish Government, the Single Market has no costs worth mentioning and many benefits. It uses any economic arguments that come to hand to support continued Single Market membership, but does not bother to critically evaluate them, since their reasons for remaining in the Single Market do not appear to be primarily economic. Any negative data, that might prompt a sensible policymaker to pause and carefully examine the implications of continued membership, such as the low growth of Scottish exports to it, or the EU's dismal record of negotiating effective trade agreements, or its catastrophic levels of unemployment since 1993, is simply ignored.

The rather perfunctory economic arguments and citations in this policy statement have attracted less attention than the various ingenious and imaginative proposals to enable Scotland to remain a member of the Single Market, while the rest of the UK exits. These have been dismissed on various grounds; because of the absurdity of the 'invisible border' between the Scotland and England, or the improbable idea that the EU or EFTA would open negotiations with a sub-state, or that the EU would admit this sub-state with a public sector deficit of 9.5 per cent. This is even worse than its present basket case, Greece, which has a deficit of 7.3 per cent. Moreover, would they accept a new member which shares the currency of a non-member, with which it has an 'invisible border' and freedom of movement and free trade.[22]

If the economic arguments are thin and perfunctory, these proposed rearrangements of the constitutional and treaty architecture of the EU, EFTA and the UK are high-flying, faintly comic, flights of fancy. In which the other states or supra-national entities involved are invited to be flexible and innovative, and asked to forget precedents and current concerns, in order to create one of the 'differentiated' outcomes that suits the Scottish government. The

Scottish government argues as if the present laboriously-assembled constitutional and treaty architecture of Europe was constructed in Legoland, and might be similarly reconstructed.

Not surprisingly, this has prompted some observers to suspect that the entire statement has some other purpose, and that none of the economic or political arguments are intended to persuade or convince anybody, because when they fail to change UK government policy, as they already have, the Scottish Government will have secured a tactical victory in what is for them the more important campaign for independence. Not getting their way on these issues will demonstrate that Scotland's five million people have not been treated as an equal partner by the 60 million of the three other UK nations. Any future economic problems that can be attributed to leaving the Single Market will provide more ammunition for the independence campaign. The economic rationale of this statement may be puzzling and incoherent, but its political rationale is quite clear. Mrs May's decision to leave the Single Market means its mission has been half accomplished, though the campaign will run through the negotiations and after Brexit.

Notes

1. A key decision is taken, but many questions remain

1   'There are millions of jobs which are impacted by the ability to trade with Europe, and thousands of businesses would be thrown into turmoil if we left… If we left the average family would end up spending £450 a year more in goods and services.' http://www.libdems.org.uk/europe-why-remain

2   Scottish Government, *Scotland's Place in Europe*, Edinburgh, 2016. 'Minister pleads with May to keep Britain in single market', Dec 26 2016. http://www. thetimes.co.uk/article/minister-pleads-with-may-to-keep-britain-in-single-market-2fc975vdp

3   http://www.cbi.org.uk/news/cbi-signs-open-letter-to-government-on-brexit-negotiations/

4   Wolfgang Münchau, 'Would it actually matter if we left the EU? There is a case for Britain remaining a member of the European Union, but it has little to do with economics', *FT*, 18th June 2015; 'Europe's dowry is not weighed in pounds and pence', *FT* 6th July 2014; 'Lord Lawson is right – Britain does not need Europe', *FT*, 12th May 2013.

5   Martin Wolf, 'Theresa May limbers up for a hard Brexit' *FT*, 20th September 2016.

2. There has been no authoritative UK analysis

1   European Parliament, 'Can we measure the performance of the Single Market?', June 2014:
http://www.europarl.europa.eu/RegData/etudes/ATAG/2014/536298/IPOL_ATA(2014)536298_EN.pdf.

2   www.journalisted.com- The only empirical evidence he chose to cite or discuss in the 198 articles was on 9th March 2004, to show that immigration from Eastern Europe would not be an issue for the UK, and on 15th December 2005, to show that UK per capita income and productivity trailed behind several other member countries.

3   Ken Clarke, 'It Is Time to put the European Case More Strongly', *Social Europe Journal*, 31st January 2013. The transcript of a speech by Ken Clarke at the launch of the Centre for British Influence through Europe delivered on 30th January 2013, http://www.social-europe.eu/2013/01

4   And 37 per cent of services. There is, however, limited data on services exports under the Common Market, or the early years of the Single Market, so we cannot say whether that is also a declining proportion.

5   Vector auto regression models project forward existing trends. They are, in effect, an extrapolation of multiple interdependent variables, and therefore, as David Blake put it, 'incapable of identifying and predicting the consequences of a structural change that has not been previously observed in the historical data used to calibrate the model.' Gravity models are based on the proposition that trade flows between two countries are proportional to their GDP and inversely proportional to their distance from one another. However, many other economic variables may be added to GDP, such as price levels and exchange rates, and other geographic and cultural variables, such as common borders, language, or legal system, or an earlier colonial relationship, to the distance variable. They try to measure all the factors that determine the level of exports between two countries and isolate the impact of trade agreements or EU and Single Market membership.

6   Although it did footnote, on pp.116, a study published shortly before its own: Nicholas Crafts, 'The growth effects of EU membership for the UK: a review of the evidence', SMF (2016).

3.   Untrustworthy estimates from the Treasury

1   Martin Wolf, 26th May 2016, 14th June 2016 and 28th June 2016.

2   Wolfgang Münchau, 'If Brexit wins out, let Britain go in peace', *FT*, 12th June 2016.

3   David Blake, 'Measurement without Theory: On the extraordinary abuse of economic models in the EU Referendum debate', Cass Business School, City University, 9th June 2016 http://www.cass.city.ac.uk/__data/assets/pdf_file/0007/320758/BlakeReviewsTreasuryModels.pdf

4   The three academic estimates cited in the Treasury's analysis are listed in the appendix with links to access them online. *HM Treasury analysis: the long-term economic impact of EU membership and the alternatives. HM Government*, April 2016, hereafter HMT Analysis (2016).

5   One standard error finds a boost to trade in goods of between 105.0 per cent and 125.7 per cent and for services between 12.3 per cent and 30.5 per cent. Calculated based on coefficients in Table A.3 (p.165), the 115 per cent boost is mentioned on p.163. *ibid.*

6   Fournier, J. et al. (2015), "Implicit Regulatory Barriers in the EU Single Market: New Empirical Evidence from Gravity Models", OECD Economics Department Working Papers, No. 1181, OECD Publishing. http://dx.doi.org/10.1787/5js7xj0xckf6-en

7   There is abundant evidence of a marked contrast in the trade intensity of the eastern and western EU which the Treasury declined to mention for example p.8, Fournier, OECD, op.cit.

8   FOI release, Treasury analysis of third party assessments of cost-benefit analyses of EU membership

Organisation: HM Treasury, 1st December 2010, 'EU Membership and Trade' https://www.gov.uk/government/uploads/system/uploads/attachment_ data/file/220968/foi_eumembership_trade.pd

9 pp.50-51, *ibid.*

10 Just a few months before, the Treasury had decided to help out in the Scottish referendum campaign by predicting that Scottish trade with the rest of the UK would decline by 80 per cent, which is as ridiculous a forecast as one is likely to find.

11 Calculations based on IMF DOTS UK export data with CAGR calculated in real terms using 1973 US dollar values (accessed at data.imf.org on 06/11/2016)

12 IMF Direction of Trade Statistics (accessed at data.imf.org on 04/05/2016), pp.28-29, Burrage, 2014, op.cit.

13 IMF Direction of Trade Statistics (accessed at data.imf.org on 06/11/2016)

14 HM Treasury, *Submissions on EMU from leading academics*, EMU Study, 2003 www.hm-treasury.gov.uk HM Treasury EMU and trade: EMU study, 2003 http://webarchive.nationalarchives.gov.uk/

UK Membership of the Single Currency: An Assessment of the Five Economic Tests, Cm 5776, HM Treasury, 2003.

15 They are spelt out in the main Treasury report but also separately in *Alternatives to membership: possible models for the United Kingdom outside the European Union*, HM Government (March 2016).

https://www.gov.uk/government/publications/alternatives-to-membership-possible-models-for-the-united-kingdom-outside-the-european-union

4. An extrapolation – what might have happened without the Single Market?

1 In order to compare a constant, the number of member countries, the three other founder members of the Single Market, Greece, Portugal and Spain, have been included – backdated to 1973.

2 The non-EU OECD countries are Australia, Canada, Chile, Israel, South Korea, Mexico, New Zealand, Switzerland and the United States. For details and other similar extrapolations see pp.79-88, Michael Burrage, *Myth and Paradox of the Single Market*, Civitas, 2015.

5. Top 40 fastest-growing goods exporters to the Single Market

1 For a more detailed account pp.21-27, Michael Burrage, *Where's the Insider Advantage?*, Civitas, London 2014.

2 p.23, *ibid.*

3 The later entrants, from 2004 onward, to the EU and the Single Market from eastern and southern Europe were entirely excluded from these comparator groups because they joined the OECD and the EU and Single Market at different points during the period under review. If the 2004 entrants had been included in the OECD figures until they gained EU membership, the

CAGR of OECD members (excluding EU countries) would have risen to 3.7 per cent and total growth would have stood at 121 per cent, well above the CAGR and total growth for the EU15 exports to each other.

6. How have exporters to the EU under WTO rules performed?

1 One further weakness of the Treasury analysis is that it never explained why the boost to the trade of EEA members, who it assures us the same access as full members, should be so much smaller.

2 http://www.cbi.org.uk/news/cbi-signs-open-letter-to-government-on-brexit-negotiations/

3 BBC Radio 4 *Today* programme, 18th January 2017.

4 To 11 members rather than 12, because in this analysis we hope to see how the UK compares with various kinds of non-member relationship, and it must therefore again be treated it as an outsider, exporting to the other 11 members. To preserve comparability, it must also be excluded from the exports of the 24 non-members. The EU mean, including the UK, is included as a measure of the rate of growth of intra-EU exports, but there too, of course, exports can only be to eleven other members.

5 Iceland's exports were not large enough to be included, but see table below.

8. A synoptic view of trading with the EU under four different relationships

1 Korea is included as it traded under WTO rules for most of the period discussed, with a trade agreement only coming into effect in 2011.

2 pp.164-5, Annex A – Modelling openness, *HMT Analysis* (2016), *op.cit*

3 One might say more about this, but this is not the place. The publication of this analysis was highly irresponsible and unworthy both of the then chancellor and of a respected department of state. The only reason for drawing attention to it is that HMT might continue to provide similarly flawed estimates during the Brexit negotiations, with unfortunate consequences.

4 See chapter 1.

9. How has UK fared when exporting under WTO rules?

1 The 111 countries are those countries without a bilateral trade treaty for which the UK reports export data to the IMF.

2 The 62 countries do not include EFTA members, Switzerland, Norway and Iceland, nor do they include Korea, since the agreement with Korea only came into force in 2011. Apart from being the second largest economy with which the EU has concluded an agreement, the agreement was followed by a rapid increase in UK exports to Korea. Hence, when included, there is a sharp spike in the bilateral treaty countries from 2013.

10. Scotch versus Bourbon: exports of an EU member and a 'most favoured nation'

1   Two striking examples are discussed in Chapter 11.

2   *Review of the Balance of Competences between the United Kingdom and the European Union: Trade and Investment* https://www.gov.uk/government/consultations/review-of-uk-and-eu-balance-of-competences-call-for-evidence-on-trade-and-investment (RBOC)

3   'RBOC: Consultation on Internal Market: Free Movement of Goods', Scotch Whisky Association comments: https://www.gov.uk/government/uploads/system/uploads/attachment_data/file/278520/ScotchWhiskyAssociation.pdf

4   United Nations Commodity Trade Statistics Database (COMTRADE) HS code 2208.30. www.comtrade.un.org.

5   Appendix II looks at how the role of trade associations could develop post-Brexit by using evidence to inform and encourage UK trade policies as part of reformed trade intelligence network.

6   http://www.scotch-whisky.org.uk/news-publications/news/brexit-what-now-for-scotch-whisky/

7   It actually cites these figures the wrong way around as if 60 Scottish firms accounted for 100 per cent of Scottish exports. pp. 2-3, The Scottish Parliament Economy, Jobs & Fair Work Committee Economic Impact of Leaving the EU: http://www.scdi.org.uk/images/document/PDFs-2016/SCDI-Submission-ScotParl-Inq-on-Economic-Impact-of-Leaving-EU-Nov16.pdf The original data source for this item and yet another gravity model estimate about a hard Brexit are discussed in Appendix III.

8   John Boothman, 'Hard Brexit a Scots job 'disaster', *The Sunday Times*, 18th December 2016.

11. Strange Brexiteer arguments against trading under WTO rules

1   http://www.eureferendum.com/documents/flexcit.pdf

2   Christopher Booker, 'The Three Brexiteers are overlooking a crucial detail on trade', Daily Telegraph, 10th September 2016.

3   The UK procedure is described in https://www.gov.uk/government/publications/notice-117-authorised-economic-operator/notice-117-authorised-economic-operator. See para 1.8 An EORI (Economic Operator & Registration Identification) number is a preliminary requirement https://www.gov.uk/eori

4   pp.118-120, World Customs Organization, *Compendium of Authorized Economic Operator Programmes*, 2016 edition http://www.wcoomd.org/

5   The EU website directory of companies with AEO status in the EU, saying what type it is, and the date and member country of issue came, into operation on 1st January 2017: http://ec.europa.eu/taxation_customs/dds2/eos/aeo_consultation. Since HMRC supplies them with the UK names,

repatriating it, preferably with links to every other such directory around the world, will hardly be a difficult or costly. In due course, the WCO itself might be persuaded to launch a world-wide site.

6   The 111 countries are those countries without a bilateral trade treaty for which the UK reports export data to the IMF. Source: IMF Direction of Trade statistics (accessed at data.imf.org on 06/11/2016)

12. Does a single market in services exist?

1   Fabienne Ilzkovitz et al, European Economy, Economic Papers, N° 271 January 2007, 'Steps towards a deeper economic integration: the Internal Market in the 21st century, A contribution to the Single Market Review European Commission', Directorate-General For Economic and Financial Affairs, ISSN 1725-3187, http://ec.europa.eu/ economy_finance/

2   The closest to an updated measure is the EU Single Market website/ Single Market Scoreboard/Performance per member state, which gives the goods and services intra-EU trade as a per cent of GDP of each. The current (2014) UK entries are 10.1 per cent in goods and 4 per cent in services meaning, it says, that UK trade in goods is the least integrated in the Single Market, and in services the second least integrated, and both fell since 2013. Only Italy is less integrated in services. Luxembourg and Ireland are the most integrated. No historical, mean or aggregate or extra-EU figures are given. http://ec.europa.eu/internal_market/scoreboard/performance_by_member_state/united_kingdom/index

3   pp.165-170, Michael Burrage, *The Eurosceptic's Handbook*, Civitas, 2016.

4   ITC Trade Map http://www.trademap.org/

5   Dominic Johnson, 'I've fallen out of love with Europe until the trading rules are changed', *Daily Telegraph*, 27th September 2015. See also Open Europe and New City Initiative, 'Asset management in Europe: The case for reform', July 2015: http://openeurope.org.uk/intelligence/economic-policy-andtrade/asset-management-in-europe-the-case-for-reform/

6   RBOC, Trade and Investment, 2013, *op.cit.*

7   p.320 Business for Britain, *Change or Go*, 2016

8   Its actual words were 'any UK discussion with the EU (bilaterally, on the basis of mutual recognition and equivalence) could lead to progress on a single financial market, at least as it pertains to the UK, above and beyond what is currently in play.' Shanker Singham, Brexit and Financial Services, Myths and Realities, Legatum Institute, September 2016, http://www.li.com/programmes/special-trade-commission

9   Accessible at http://www.oecd.org/tad/services-trade/services-trade-restrictiveness-index.htm

10 pp .1294-1452, Comprehensive Economic and Trade Agreement Between Canada, of the One Part, and the European Union and its Member States (CETA) 2016

13. Top 40 fastest-growing service exporters to the EU28

1   Though the Treasury blithely refers to services data 'for 195 countries since 1981', a glance at the file shows that reasonable coverage of even a dozen countries only begins in the late 1990s. p.164, Table A2. This is yet another breach of research etiquette.

2   These rankings are not prepared in exactly the same manner as those of goods, since the exports to the EU do not exclude the UK, and therefore the UK's own export growth is not to the same number of countries as all the rest.

15. Have Swiss services exports suffered outside the Single Market?

1   Some examples: 'Switzerland has no guaranteed access to the EU market in financial services, and in particular no access to the financial services passport… only some services sectors are covered, such as non-life insurance and public procurement. Switzerland has limited guaranteed market access for professional services, including accountancy and legal services… Swiss firms do not enjoy the flexibility of UK firms in how they deliver their services in the EU, and do not enjoy the same rights in respect of establishing these subsidiaries… Switzerland's 'third-country' status, and the barriers to EU market access this entails, is likely to be one reason for the large amount of financial services FDI from Switzerland into the UK. In 2014, 26.4% of European investment in UK financial services came from Switzerland.' pp.42,90,105, *HMT Analysis* (2016) *op.cit.*

2   ITC Trade Map http://www.trademap.org/Index.aspx

16. The big 'known unknown': passports, clearing and other financial services

1   Clearing houses or central counterparties (CCP) reduce the risks and costs of transactions in numerous financial markets by acting as intermediaries for both buyers and sellers.

2   Philip Stafford, Why the EU's euro clearing Brexit threat may never happen, *Financial Times*, June 29, 2016

3   Oliver Wyman, 'The Impact of The UK's Exit from the EU on the UK-based Financial Services Sector', September, 2016; Open Europe, 'How the UK's financial services sector can continue thriving after Brexit', October 2016.

4   Moreover, as Reynolds points out, many EU-related activities are not in fact cross-border at all. Barnabas Reynolds, 'Brexit: Continuity of current arrangements for banks and investment banks', http://www.lawyersforbritain.org/

5   p.30, Open Europe, op.cit. OW's observations on these two sub-sectors, incidentally, add credence to the argument above that a single market in services barely exists.

6 ITC Trade Map http://www.trademap.org/Country_SelServiceCountry. Some of these figures are not the same as the ONS versions.

7 p.10, *The Government's Review of the Balance of Competences Between the United Kingdom and the European Union, Internal Market: Synoptic Review, response by the City of London Corporation*, March 2013

8 ITC Trade Map http://www.trademap.org/

9 p.8, *ibid.*

10 These, and some still to come into force, are listed in the Legatum Institute Briefing of September 2016, followed by a list of 'the present gaps in respect of key financial services where there is no passport or equivalence regime.' Singham, 2016, *op.cit.*

11 For a very informed account Reynolds, 2016, *op.cit.*

12 The services in which there is a 'compelling mutual interest' to reach a Brexit solution are itemized in Shanker A. Singham and Victoria Hewson, Financial Services Briefing, Special Trade Commission, Legatum Institute, October 2016, www.li.com, EU providers have passports for deposit taking and lending p.9, for investment services, p.22, and for insurance, p.26.

13 Among other things, the OECD Code specifically prohibits beggar-thy-neighbour policies and discriminatory treatment of investors in other countries, in particular discrimination based on residency. In March 2016, adhering countries agreed to strengthen the Code. http://www.oecd.org/investment/investment-policy/codes.htm

14 Reynolds, 2016, *op.cit.*

15 John Tizard, 'Clearing houses should not be a bargaining tool in Brexit talks, 'Relocating euro-denominated clearing from London is costly, legally complex and technically risky', *Financial Times*, 10th July 2016, and Stafford 2016, *op.cit.*

16 By contrast, the outstandingly informed, and consistently optimistic, contributions to the debate by Philip Stafford, John Tizard and Barnabas Reynolds, op.cit are never mentioned in news reports.

17 An earlier attempt to require that euro-denominated instruments were cleared within the eurozone was blocked by the ECJ because the ECB did not have the authority to impose a territorial restriction of this kind. According to the FT, urged by the Bank of France, the European Commission is currently planning to give them this authority before Brexit. 'EU prepares rule changes to target City's euro clearing', *Financial Times*, 15th December 2016.

18 The Centre for Aviation has several extended analyses of the complications and difficulties that might arise, marred only by its acceptance of the Treasury analysis discussed above. It is of the view that it is unlikely that the UK will be excluded from ECAA but that there would be fewer problems and uncertainties about this if the UK was to remain a member of the Single Market. http://centreforaviation.com/analysis/brexit-up-in-the-air-implications-for-aviation-if-the-uk-votes-to-leave-the-european-union-262860

17. Other dashed hopes and unfounded claims: the Single Market in retrospect

1   HM Government, The United Kingdom and the European Communities, White Paper, Cmnd 4715, 1971, p.16

2   'Commission of the European Communities', 'Europe 1992: The overall challenge', Brussels, 1988, Paolo Cecchini et al., SEC (88)524. http:// aei.pitt. edu/3813/.

3   Ali M. El-Agraa and Brian Ardy, The European Union: Economics and Policies, Seventh Edition, (Cambridge University Press, 2011) pp.110-112. They later refer to it as 'a political success'.

4   pp.31-33, Barry Eichengreen and Andrea Boltho, 'The Economic Impact of European Integration', Centre for Economic Policy Research Paper No. 6820, 2008, www.cepr.org/pubs/dps/DP6820.asp. However, they do say that 'the welfare losses arising from the CAP' have to be set against the estimated gain in EU GDP growth during the Common Market, which were 'almost certainly substantial for the United Kingdom.'

5   p.91, Hugo Dixon, The In/Out Question: why Britain should stay in the EU and fight to make it better, Scampstonian, 2014. He too didn't tell us how much this jewel cost.

6   pp.121, 131, 138, 142, HMT, 2016, op.cit.

7   pp.151-155, Annex A Modelling Openness, HMT Analysis (2016), 2016.

8   The Sunday Times Economics Editor seemed to think this comparison in itself made the case for EU membership. 'The figures spoke for themselves... Since the single market came into being, growth in Britain's per capita gross domestic product has exceeded that of America.' David Smith, These rocky roads all lead back to the 'leave' vote, The Sunday Times, 25th December 2016.

9   The contrast between Ireland and the UK raises fascinating questions. Since FDI promotes productivity growth why is it that the UK, with a distinctively high rate of inward investment, as the following section shows, still lags so badly in growth of productivity?

10   pp.79-80, Burrage, 2014, op.cit. Research about the determinants of investors' decisions, and the debate at the time of the debate on euro entry is examined at some length in this paper

11   pp.75-90, 108-122, Burrage, 2014, op.cit.

12   pp.2, 174-175, HMT Analysis (2016), op.cit.

13   Fabienne Ilzkovitz, Adriaan Dierx, Viktoria Kovacs and Nuno Sousa, European Economy, Economic Papers, N° 271 January 2007, 'Steps towards a deeper economic integration: the Internal Market in the 21st century, A contribution to the Single Market Review', European Commission, Directorate-General for Economic and Financial Affairs, ISSN 1725-3187, http://ec.europa.eu/economy_finance/index_en.htm

14   Michael Gestrin, 'International investment in Europe: A canary in the coal mine?', OECD Investment Insights, November 2014. http://www.oecd.org/ investment/investment-policy/InvestmentInsights-Nov2014.pdf

15 Although Luxembourg, Belgium and the Netherlands record high per capita inward stock, they have been omitted because they appear to include a high proportion of Special Purpose Financial Entities (SPEs) as distinct from authentic FDI to establish and run a business under the control of the investor. See pp.86-90, Burrage, 2014, *op.cit.*

16 The graph exaggerates both the stock and the growth since the EU15 includes the three countries with very high proportions of SPEs.

17 P.182, *The Eurosceptic's Handbook*, Burrage, Civitas, 2016

18 The first *ex post* assessment of bilateral trade agreements was, according to the European Commission, Itaqa Sarl, 'Evaluation of the economic impact of the Trade Pillar of the EU Chile Association Agreement', Final report, for the European Commission, Directorate General for Trade, March 2012: http://trade.ec.europa.eu/doclib/docs/2012/ august/tradoc_149881. However Copenhagen Economics, 'Ex-Post Assessment of Six EU Free Trade Agreements, An econometric assessment of their impact on trade', prepared for the European Commission, DG Trade, February 2011: http://trade. ec.europa.eu/doclib/docs/2011/may/tradoc_147905 seems to be considered as a pilot. Neither study isolates the impact on individual member countries.

19 Treasury analysis echoed this positive assessment, and by adding together the EU itself and all the countries with which the EU *has opened negotiations* was able to conclude that '82 per cent of the UK's current exports will be with either the EU or to markets with which the EU has external trade deals. (Italics added) p.108, *op.cit.* The 6.1 per cent of all UK goods exports and 1.8 per cent of all UK services exports mentioned above refer to agreements in force in 2016, and exclude both the EU itself and EFTA.

20 Mixed competence agreements are those which extend beyond the EU's common commercial policy or treaty amendments to it. Generally speaking they are those having a services element, or until the Treaty of Lisbon those dealing with intellectual property. For a detailed commentary and the 1994 ECJ decision on mixed competence http://www.lawyersforbritain.org/int-trade.shtml

21 The Investment for Growth and Jobs, item 1.2 in the EU Budget, is for the most part administered by the D-G for Employment, Social Affairs & Inclusion. It has increased from €36.9 billion in 2007 to €54.4 billion in 2014, and totalled just under €346 billion over the eight years.

22 In a poll of its readers, a majority of whom one imagines are Leave voters, 60% of the 17,798 who responded expressed a preference for staying in the Single Market. 'Should Theresa May fight to keep Britain in the Single Market?', *Daily Telegraph*, 26th October 2016.

19. Conclusions

1 The underlying figures are taken from the EC Financial Statement and refer to the years 2000-2014 pp.85-89, Burrage, *Handbook, op.cit*

20. Notes on the negotiations

1   This seems to be the position of the Labour leader. 'Jeremy Corbyn says UK should reject key aspects of single market after Brexit: Labour leader wants full access to EU markets for British firms but would seek to ditch certain directives and obligations', *The Guardian*, 7th September 2016.

2   'We will introduce, in the next Queen's Speech, a Great Repeal Bill that will remove the European Communities Act from the statute book.' The Secretary of State for Exiting the EU later explained that this meant that 'EU law will be transposed into domestic law, wherever practical, on exit day.' 'Brexit begins: Theresa May takes axe to EU laws', *Daily Telegraph* 2nd October 2016; Theresa May to trigger article 50 by end of March 2017, *The Guardian*, 2nd October 2016.

3   pp.549-711, Protocol on rules of origin and origin procedures, CETA, *op.cit* http://trade.ec.europa.eu/doclib/docs/2014/september/tradoc_152806.pdf

4   Though 0.35 percentage points lower than the EU mean. Chapter 11

5   Given that the attempt to punish the City of London by restricting the clearing of euro-denominated financial instruments to the eurozone is already under way. fn 78, *supra*.

6   One cannot assume that all those on the EU side are, like M. Barnier, working for a speedy, smooth and orderly departure. According to various unnamed informants in the Commission, Martin Selmayr, chief-of-staff of European Commission president Jean-Claude Juncker, 'is a "believer" and he believes a destructive Brexit is the best way to keep Europe together... The member states are divided and distracted and the reality is that Brexit is not their number one priority – which leaves Selmayr free to constantly degrade the mood of the talks at the margin. No-one should underestimate him.' Peter Foster, 'Revealed: the 'monster' EU hardliner accused of trying to 'blow up' Brexit by poisoning the negotiations', *Daily Telegraph*, 18th December 2016.

7   There is here, I suppose, some scope for the UK to cherry pick, but it is difficult to see how the EU could stop it, except by turning away a contributor, and useful partner, in one or other agency or programme.

8   House of Commons Library, 'Leaving the EU', Research Paper 13/42, 1 July 2013. Article 3 of protocol 4 of the ECHR prohibits the collective expulsion of aliens. http://www.echr.coe.int/Documents/Convention_ENG.pdf

9   Revealed: How Theresa May's fight for British expat rights was met with silence from EU leaders, *Daily Telegraph*, 17th December 2016.

10 The main reason for coming to the UK in the year ending June 2016 was, for 31 per cent of EU nationals, to 'look for work', and 81,000, reported that they did not have a job to go to, whereas only 10 per cent of non-EU nationals came to look for work, and 24,000 reported that they did not have a job to go. Of the 105,000 people who came looking for work, but did not have a job to go to, therefore, 77 per cent were from the EU. p.12, Office for National Statistics Statistical bulletin, Migration Statistics Quarterly Report: December 2016. https://www.ons.gov.uk/people

11 The Brussels correspondent of *The Times* noted that 'no European country, during bilateral talks with EU negotiators, has front-loaded with a demand

for free movement rights for new migrant workers seeking access to Britain's labour market', '£60bn divorce demand could wreck May's hopes of a deal' The Times, 16th November 2016.

12 As may be seen from the comments reported in CBI, 'Making a Success of Brexit A whole-economy view of the UK-EU Negotiations', December 2016

13 Links to both, as well as the EU's own take on these procedures are given on the EU website: http://ec.europa.eu/trade/policy/accessing-markets/dispute-settlement/

Appendix I. Comments on *HM Treasury analysis: the long-term economic impact of EU membership and the alternatives*

1 For example p.8, Fournier et al, 2015, *op.cit*

2 pp.164-5, Annex A – Modelling openness, *HMT Analysis* (2016), *op.cit.*

3 pp.21-27, Michael Burrage, *Where's the Insider Advantage*, Civitas, 2014.

4 Numerous examples are discussed and cited in Scott L. Baier, et al, 'Do economic integration agreements actually work? Issues in understanding the causes and consequences of the growth of regionalism', pp. 461-497, *The World Economy*, Vol. 31, No.4, 2008.

5 'the coefficient on EEA membership is not statistically significant, and a priori it seems unlikely that services trade would be so negatively affected by EEA membership. Furthermore, the fact that only two countries have joined the EEA and that the time span of available data is shorter means the sample size is Single Marketaller... when calibrating the total trade impact that enters into the quantitative analysis in Section 3 of the main document, the EEA effect for services was set to zero. p.164, *op.cit.*

6 http://www.publications.parliament.uk/ 9th June 2003.

7 Reuven Glick and Andrew K. Rose, Currency Unions and Trade: A Post?EMU Mea Culpa *Revised Draft: June 16, 2015 http://faculty.haas.berkeley.edu/arose/Glick2.pdf

8 Which they must have seen, since they cite the website on which the mea culpa appeared. They sidestep the methodological issue by saying that Rose's original dataset meant his estimates 'could not be applied to EU countries', as if the econometric methodology obstacle he identified were solely an inappropriate dataset. fn16,18, pp.159, 164.

Appendix II. On the role of trade associations in a post-Brexit trade intelligence network

1 They may perhaps be informing the Department for Exiting the EU or the Department on International Trade, and prefer not to publish their findings, though if so, one must hope that their evidence is of a rather higher standard than that presented in submissions to the FCO Balance of Competences Review.

2   CBI, 'Making a Success of Brexit A whole-economy view of the UK-EU Negotiations', December 2016.

3   'Review of the Balance of Competences between the United Kingdom and the European Union; Trade and Investment'. Submission of the Society of Motor Manufacturers and Traders. The volume is unpaginated. https://www.gov.uk/government/consultations/review-of-uk-and-eu-balance-of-competences-call-for-evidence-on-trade-and-investment.

4   Mirror data give export data of a country not from its own records, but from the imports reported by its partner. It is commonly measured c.i.f, whereas exports are usually reported f.o.b. That accounts for some of the discrepancies between the two figures on these products, but by no means all.

Appendix III. On the Scottish Government's puzzling enthusiasm for membership of the Single Market

1   Scottish Government, *Scotland's Place in Europe*, Edinburgh, 2016.

2   'Scotland's pro-Brexit fishing federation warns ministers over EU stance', *The Guardian*, 4th July 2016.

3   The footnote given refers to an August press release: http://news.gov.scot/news/brexit-research-shows-economic-risk-to-scotland

4   In fact it suggested that the losses over the long run, which it emphasised but did not put a date on, might be 60 per cent in services and between 35 and 44 percent in goods. Monique Ebell, 'Assessing the Impact of Trade Agreements', NIESR National Institute Economic Review No. 238, November 2016, http://www.niesr.ac.uk/publications/assessing-impact-tradeagreements-trade#

5   This model makes predictions about the UK's transition from full membership to some form of FTA, with data referring to a single year, 2014, and essentially seeks to mathematically simulate Brexit by comparing the trade of existing EU members with that of nine countries having FTA relationship with the EU in that year, as if never having joined was identical to withdrawal. She does not explain why she omits to mention or consider the only country that has exited the EU – Greenland. Her own concluding account of the limitations of her analysis is worth reading.

6   Table 1,6 Scottish Government, Export Statistics Scotland, http://www.gov.scot/Topics/Statistics/Browse/Economy/Exports/ESSPublication/ESSExcel David Bell, *The economy: how closely is our economy aligned with the EU?*, 2016, http://www.centreonconstitutionalchange.ac.uk/sites/default/files/DB.pdf

7   Policy Submission to The Scottish Parliament, Economy, Jobs & Fair Work Committee, 'Economic Impact of Leaving the EU' November 2016, www.scdi.org.uk

8   For whisky see http://www.scotch-whisky.org.uk/news-publications/news/brexit-what-now-for-scotch-whisky/#.WJZb2tKLSJA and for petroleum and refined products http://www.europedia.moussis.eu/books/Book_2/6/19/02/04/?all=1

9   The total value of Scotland's exports of agriculture, forestry and fishing to the EU in 2014 was £185 million

10 Export Statistics Scotland, op.cit. 'At the very least' because the Global Connections Survey points out, many respondents declined to give any figures because they could not split their rest of the UK business from that in Scotland alone. p.14, Scottish Government, Statistical Bulletin Economy Series, *Scotland's Global Connections Survey 2013 Estimating Exports from Scotland* 26th January 2015 http://www.gov.scot/Resource/0046/00469028.pdf

11 Paragraph 106, And the Scottish Council for Development and Industry did not show why trading under WTO rules would be, as it claimed, 'seriously detrimental' to Scottish firms. It expressed its opinion. Paragraph 13, Policy Statement, op.cit

12 Direct costs are mentioned incidentally when referring to the benefits of remaining in the EEA, but only to point out that they would fall significantly. Paragraph 103, *Scotland's Place in Europe*

13 Bell, 2016, *op.cit.*

14 Paragraphs 38, 69 and 88, *Scotland's Place in Europe.*

15 The best starting point is the xl document giving the data of national contributions and receipts for 15 years at EU expenditure and revenue 2000-2014 http://ec.europa.eu/budget/financialreport/2014/annex/2/index_en.html. They are examined in detail pp.85-89, Michael Burrage, **The Eurosceptic's Handbook**, Civitas, London, 2016, On pp. 248-258 grants for academic research are examined in detail, since of all recipient groups they are most determined to pretend the EU is their benefactor, rather than the UK taxpayer.

16 'There can be no doubt that the life each individual in our country is enriched by the cultural diversity and vibrancy that people from other EU countries bring to our neighbourhoods, our sporting teams, to the arts and our cultural life, and to our workplaces.' Paragraph 78, *Scotland's Place in Europe.*

17 Evidence submitted to the EU Home Affairs Sub-Committee by the Office for National Statistics
http://data.parliament.uk/writtenevidence/committeeevidence.svc/evidencedocument/eu-home-affairs-subcommittee/brexit-ukeu-movement-of-people/written/44746.html

18 In 2014, the population density of England was 415 per sq km, Wales 148, and Scotland 66. Within the EU, England is exceeded only by the Netherlands (501) and Malta (1352), Scotland is amongst the lowest. Only the Baltic states have less. http://ec.europa.eu/eurostat/en/web/products-datasets/-/TPS00003

19 Paragraphs 8, 9, 70, 130, 172 and footnote 46, *Scotland's Place in Europe.*

20 Paragraphs 8, 9, 34 and 70, *Scotland's Place in Europe.*

21 Paragraphs 182 and 183, *Scotland's Place in Europe.*

22 p.4, Mike Denham, *Scotland's Overspending Problem*, Taxpayers Alliance, 2016. His figures are quoting the OECD World Economic Outlook June 2016.